# UNLOCK YOUR INNER WARRIOR

By Tricia Andreassen

**Co-Authored by:**
Anna Brehm Anderson
Kate Bancroft
Chestina Parker Dowgiewicz
Jacquie Fazekas
Lydia Gates
Paula Pierce
Amanda Powell
Edward Reed
Samuel Rowland
Aarti Royan
Carlos E. Vargas
Taffiney Nolan Williams

CLPLI, LLC
www.CLPLI.com
Info@CLPLI.com

Book Versions
Ingram ISBN: 978-1-946265-24-1
eBook ISBN: 978-1-946265-25-8
KDP Paperback ISBN: 978-1-946265-26-5

Cover Design By Dara Rogers

Copyright © 2019 Creative Life Publishing & Learning Institute

All rights reserved. No part of this book may be reproduced in any form without prior written permission from the publisher. This work represents the views and opinions of the author alone. No liability in conjunction with the content or the use of ideas connected with this work is assumed by the publisher.

**THE HOLY BIBLE, NEW INTERNATIONAL VERSION®,** NIV® Copyright © 1973, 1978, 1984, 2011 by Biblica, Inc.® Used by permission. All rights reserved worldwide.

*"New International Version"* and *"NIV"* are registered trademarks of Biblica, Inc.®

*"Dr. Oz"* is a registered trademarks of OZ MEDIA LLC.

# CONTENTS

**ABOUT TRICIA ANDREASSEN**   5

**CHAPTER 1 | UNLOCKING OF THE WARRIOR**   7
by Tricia Andreassen

**CHAPTER 2 | THE WARRIOR BATTLE**   35
by Tricia Andreassen

**CHAPTER 3 | REACH BEYOND!**   51
by Anna Brehm Anderson

**CHAPTER 4 | THE HEART OF OUR FATHER**   65
by Kate Bancroft

**CHAPTER 5 | SIMPLY PUT...MY STORY, A SONG, MY PRAISE!**   81
by Chestina Parker Dowgiewicz

**CHAPTER 6 | THE JOURNEY OF AN INNER WARRIOR**   95
by Jacquie Fazekas

**CHAPTER 7 | WARRIOR COURAGE**   109
by Lydia Gates

**CHAPTER 8 | WARRIOR RECOVERY**   119
by Lydia Gates

**CHAPTER 9 | RISE UP: KINGS AND QUEENS OF GOD!**   127
by Paula Pierce

**CHAPTER 10 | THE WARRIOR STRENGTH DISCOVERED**   145
by Amanda Powell

**CHAPTER 11 | ADVERSITY: FRIEND OR FOE OF YOUR INNER WARRIOR**   159
by Edward Reed

**CHAPTER 12 | PEEL OFF THE LABEL: YOU'RE PRICELESS!**   169
by Samuel Rowland

**CHAPTER 13 | EVICT THE VICTIM, EMBRACE THE VICTOR!**   187
by Aarti Royan

**CHAPTER 14 | (YAAW) YOU ARE A WARRIOR**     **201**
by Carlos E. Vargas

**CHAPTER 15 | THE BIRTHING OF A WARRIOR**     **217**
by Taffiney Nolan Williams

**CHAPTER 16 | SONGS OF THE WARRIOR**     **231**
by Tricia Andreassen

# ABOUT TRICIA ANDREASSEN

Tricia Andreassen has a mission—a *"life calling"* she describes like this:

*"My mission is to bring teaching and strategies to breakthrough challenges, struggles, and obstacles that show up daily in our business and personal lives. Each person has a purpose and calling. I want to help as many people as possible discover what God has placed in their heart to do."*

As a young entrepreneur, Tricia bought her first real estate investment property at age nineteen, became a manager of a real estate company and continued on as National Speaker for Realtor.com where she trained real estate professionals how to market themselves on the Internet. Seeing a need in the real estate industry, Tricia started Pro Step Marketing and Advertising in grass roots fashion from the bonus room of her house and grew it into one of the most internationally recognizable companies within the real estate technology space. After almost fifteen years as a CEO and CMO she sold her company to expand her professional speaking, coaching practices, and training programs in the Christian faith. Her business book Interfusion Marketing hit #1 in less than five hours and remained on the best-seller list for fifty-nine weeks. She now is a multi best selling Author in the Christian Living genre addressing topics such as resilience, courage, hope, and more.

John Maxwell, the world's #1 ranked leadership expert, has certified Tricia as both Speaker and Coach to teach leadership, personal growth, and youth development programs. Her credentials also include an Executive Coach ACTP certification through the International Coaching Federation that positions Tricia to bring creative strategies to organizations, schools, ministry groups, and leaders from all walks of life. Her coaching practice is unique in bringing forth the strengths that lie within so they are maximized in business, in life and in relationships.

As her mission progresses, Tricia's growing life story continues to be told with a central message of persistence, resilience, and faith woven into insightful strategies that heal the soul and create breakthrough. Her passion is to creatively deliver, inspire, motivate, and to bring lasting change through writing, speaking, teaching, the arts (including songwriting) in intimate gatherings such as workshops and retreats that focus on unlocking inner warrior strength. While having a focus on the spiritual, Tricia brings this understanding into the company workforce environment through Organizational Development, Digital Marketing Campaigns, Sales Training, People Management, and DISC Behavioral Consulting.

To inquire about Tricia's speaking topics, private coaching or group programs email Warrior@MsUnstoppable.com.

## CONTACT TRICIA

- Website: www.UnstoppableWarrior.com
- LinkedIn: www.LinkedIn.com/in/TriciaAndreassen
- Facebook: www.Facebook.com/UnstoppableWarrior
- YouTube: www.UnstoppableWarriorWithin.net
- Twitter: www.Twitter.com/TriciaSings
- Books: www.TriciaAndreassenBooks.com
- Radio: www.UnlockYourInnerWarrior.com
- Songs: www.IgniteTheFireSongs.com
- Speaking Inquires: www.MsUnstoppable.com/Contact
- Retreats, Conferances, and Masterminds: www.WarriorGatherings.com

# CHAPTER 1
# UNLOCKING OF THE WARRIOR

By Tricia Andreassen

**I** still remember the day of August 22, 2014 as if it was yesterday. I was supposed to be having a good time, relaxing with my friend and our children as we enjoyed the serenity of the beach on Hilton Head Island.

However, that *vacationing feeling* couldn't have been farther from the truth, as I literally felt my heart aching; it was as if every ounce of my body and soul wanted to cocoon within itself. For the first time I can remember, I felt as if I had lost all control of my life and the need for realignment suddenly became overwhelming.

Memories began purging from my mind, I could see that everything from everywhere had been screaming at me to listen and take notice of the spiral that I was experiencing, but of course, this type *"A"* woman just wouldn't hear of it!

Oh no, I was the one that could *"take the bull by the horns and get stuff done."* I was the *"go-to"* person who could rally the troops and get them ready for battle, the one who always looked at the *"glass half full."* I have an empowerment question that I use whenever I am faced with a challenge, I ask myself, *"What's the gift in this, Tricia?"* and I press forward.

For the most part, this optimism always served me well; to be the one who always looked at the bright side of things. But, let's get real, there are times that we can't see the gift in a situation and that is where I was at in this moment on vacation in the summer of 2014.

You see, it was only eighteen months prior to this moment in which

I had committed myself into digging deeper to finish a book on business that I had been diligently working on for a year. It was within those eighteen-months from March of 2013 to August of 2014, in which areas within me were being pushed to the surface to give way to the person I have become today. It was one of many seasons of breakthrough.

The pain I felt that summer vacation on Hilton Head Island, the agony of feeling powerless within my life was because in that moment I was battling the burdens of how others saw me and the responsibility I felt to be someone else for other people; especially for my family.

Looking back with you today I have the clarity of how many times God had given me opportunities to step into all of my identity. I can see that He had been steadily knocking on my spirit, trying to get me to listen; to align with what He had called me to do, but I was just so stubborn. I was living for my outcome and drowning in that feeling of never being enough. I attempted to battle them the way I thought worked, *It was my life and I was going to live it that way! I was going to reach the goals; if it was to be, it's because it was up to me!*

These are the phrases that had powered my thoughts and actions; how self-absorbed was I?! To think that I was ever in control, holding a wand which could magically make things work the way I wanted!

Today, I finally understand the truth: I understand that we have to first take note of what our intuition is trying to tell us. Leadership expert John Maxwell has said, *"Prayer is when you talk to God. Intuition is when God is talking to you."*

With this belief and the faith to listen, we have the <u>ability</u> (and choice) to HEED the voice that is whispering (sometimes even screaming) to get our attention. And yet, we still chose to ignore it or chose to only listen when it is convenient and serves us.

That is exactly where I was in my moment of anguish on Hilton Head Island in 2014. When all of the pieces of my life, all of the flashes of my misguided decisions and the hidden secrets of my pain, left me feeling completely *BROKEN*. In this moment of complete humility, I would find it to become the only way I would give everything over to Him; the only way to get on my knees and give it **ALL** to Him.

> *"Come, let us return to the LORD. He has torn us to pieces, but he will heal us; he has injured us, but he will bind up our wounds."*
> Hosea 6:1

Prior to this surrender, I had been given many messages from my Heavenly Father. But, as a spoiled child, I only listened when it seemed relevant to me, and if I can be completely honest in this reflection, the messages were from a voice that had visited me many times within my life.

*Being baptized*

When I was just seven years old, I gave my life to Jesus and was baptized. I remember the day of my baptism so vividly; Pastor Sexton at *Dublin Church of God* held my hand as I was led into the big tub.

*"Do you know how powerful this moment is?"* He asked me.

I did, I was crying to my Heavenly Father knowing that I was chosen to be a light for him. I received the Holy Spirit when I was around this age at youth camp and can still remember laying hands on children beside me, praying for their hearts to come to Christ. Singing songs while my mom played the piano to hundreds of people, gave me the knowing of operating in my purpose, to be an encourager and worshiper felt so *right* in my spirit.

Even though these moments existed within my life, somehow, I still lost my way as anger and resentment began to surface within my heart during my late teen years. The enemy tried to plant the lies within my mind at a mere nine years old, that people just pretended to be of Jesus – and often I was shown that for many of them, there was no truth to their belief in my Lord and Savior.

*Our trailer from 6th grade to 1st year in college*

Thankfully, I could feel the anointing of my Lord when I sang. I was able to discern evil when I saw it; when I *felt* it. At this age I wasn't able to understand it but I can tell you that although I faced many fearful situations my God stayed with me. He was my comforter.

The enemy would attack me mentally, deep within my core, as my brother-in-law French kissed me when I was only nine (even though professed to know Christ and he was studying ministry); scaring me so terribly, I didn't even tell my sister (Karen) until many years later.

The first experience I remember of my resentment towards religion began to grow when I endured sexual abuse from my uncle forcing me to hold his hand and kiss him; yet when I sought solace within my parents' arms, they told me to just stay away from Him. I remember the day He came to our trailer and knocked on the door to ask my dad for forgiveness. My dad let him in, then prayed with him while I was there. The enemy used this as fuel to anger me.

Even though the people within my family were all supposed to be within the ministry, it didn't stop the physical abuse, threatening words, or yelling voices which occurred throughout those years growing up. These injustices began to haunt me and the hurt I endured for all of those years rooted deep into my core rising as a major internal battle at times. It was from my 10th grade to end of my senior year in high school when I battled the enemy in my mind. I say it was in my mind but there were physical showings of this battle in my family environment. Things that I had chosen to ignore or be in denial over slammed into my reality. The anger of those actions of someone close to me who said they were a servant of God caused resentment. The enemy worked hard on planting in me that religion was hypocritical and people would use the word *"Minister"* to hide behind their own sin. I slowly escaped God's ordained calling upon me.

## BUT GOD!

He had called me as a Warrior before I was even born into this world; throughout all of these years HIS VOICE (what I knew as my intuition) was always there, speaking into my heart. During these years He gave me signs on my life pathway.

In 4th grade, I realized I could soothe the pain of life through writing, as I wrote a book of poems and gave it to my teacher voluntarily. Again in 6th grade, I recall sitting at the piano for hours as lyrics of my own began to circulate within my mind:

*All alone*
*Here in my bedroom I'm all alone*
*I don't know what to do*
*I'm so sad*
*I just feel like crying now*

*Dressed up to sing at church*

*Music…Words…* These are the two main weapons I was given to fight for and heal that inner, injured part of myself. These weapons, coupled with performing at church and singing to an audience, filled my soul with hope during the dark places of loneliness I experienced.

One of my favorite songs I had learned to play on the piano was, *"Thank you Lord for your blessings on me."* What a powerful affirmation to speak into existence while in these moments of complete loss.

Even with these gifts, I had no idea that they were pieces of my armor. When my ten-year-old self looked into the mirror, the only reflection I could see was that of a girl in middle school, living in a twenty-three foot camper at a trailer park, trying to find her self-worth in the midst of a town filled with wealthy college professor's kids at Virginia Tech. I felt ashamed

*Our camper where I lived from 4th to 6th grade*

of where I lived and never wanted to invite friends over.

I will be direct in saying, some of my memories are fuzzy during my adolescence, most likely due to the stress I endured. I remember one occasion, crying and shaking within my 7th grade Social Studies class that my Dad had to check me out early from school. The guidance counselor asked me lots of questions trying to find out what I was feeling and what was wrong, but I never did give them a straight answer. My intuition tells me that it was the abuse from my Uncle John that one weekend, coupled with my dad's continuous fight with depression that brought this on. At that time in my life, I found that the memories and deep feelings had been coming to the surface more often for me to address.

I believe it is because of this powerful affirmation that I have committed myself to, *"I am a Warrior and my scars have made me the woman I am today, to make a difference in people's lives."*

*Dublin, Virginia Church of God where I was saved*

Yes, my Lord had hard wired me with the DNA to persevere and to believe in something more than I could see in the moment. God used music to help me through all of these times, in 8th grade after returning from youth camp, He began to unlock my voice, it is then that I felt called to preach to my mom's church congregation. I remember the spirit of God on me like fire igniting every part of me. Right around the same time, in 9th grade, I attended a church revival. At the revival for the first time I experienced a southern Virginian woman who spoke in tongues, she was from a background where I am certain she had never studied Latin. However, in that service she said a string of Latin words that I understood only one phrase and as soon as she said it my whole body felt complete *"Awe."*

On the drive home, I asked my mom, *"Did you know that she was speaking Latin?"* I don't remember what my mom said or how she responded but I do remember that I translated it to her.

*"She said in Latin, 'Sing to the Lord.' I know that because we are studying this sheet music in Chorus right now!"* I exclaimed.

As I am able to understand more clearly now, I know God was giving me this message: *Sing to The Lord.* This solidified in my heart then and just as strongly today, that I must never compromise the gifts of my songwriting and singing on my life's journey, it is most definitely a part of my everyday purpose and calling.

I STAND STRONG WITH YOU ALL IN THE PROCLAMATION OF THESE WORDS:

*"WITH GOD IN US WE ARE UNSTOPPABLE. WE MUST CONTINUE AND GO FORTH BECAUSE OUR VOICE MATTERS."* I am affirming this with you, right now.

Even in high school as I sat in my Spanish class doodling and writing lyrics within my notebook.

At fourteen I wrote these words:

> *"I decided long ago never to walk in anyone's shadow*
> *If I fail if I succeed at least I lived as I believe*
> *no matter what they take from me*
> *they can't take away my dignity*
>
> *because the greatest love of all is happening to me*
> *learning to love yourself*
> *it is the greatest love of all*
> *and if by chance that special place*

*that you've been dreaming of
leads you to a lonely place
find your strength in love.*

- Whitney Houston, Greatest Love of All [1]

Even then, God was with me; he had given me the gifts that needed to be shared with the world, but I just didn't see it.

Yet.

I had mistakenly allowed these lyrics to train me that everything within this life was within my hands, instead of me being in the palm of **HIS**.

> *"See, I have engraved you on the palms of my hands; your walls are ever before me."*
> Isaiah 49:16

Christian lyrics by Sandi Patti also poured over my spirit in high school and I memorized all of her songs. They ministered to me greatly to remind me that God was wonderful and I should behold him always. My early teen years I was asked to sing one of my favorite songs to sing; *Because Of Who You Are*.

*You spoke the words and all the worlds came into order
You waved your hands and planets filled the empty skies
You placed the woman and the man inside the garden
And though they fell they found compassion in your eyes
Oh Lord I stand amazed at the wonder of your deeds
And yet a greater wonder brings me to my knees*

*Lord I praise you, because of who you are
Not for all the mighty things that you have done
Lord, I worship you, because of who you are
You're all the reason that I need to voice my praise* [2]

Even in all of those times in my life I let the enemy in. Recrafting myself to seek success and escape the family issues that seemed to follow me. Through college and into my adulthood I ran as far from God as possible. I admit, I did things to defy Him because I was so angry of what I had learned over the years about my family history and all the terrible secrets. It was the way for the enemy to take me as far away from God as possible.

Even so, while I practiced real estate in my twenty's, He used people in my life to deliver me and show me His everlasting commitment and love for me. I know that now and those stories could be a book itself, but what I can tell you is this, God will never leave you or forsake you, even in your most shameful sin, He loves you so much and just wants you to come back to Him.

> *"Keep your lives free from the love of money and be content with what you have, because God has said,*
> *Never will I leave you; never will I forsake you."*
> Hebrews 13:5

In March of 2013, it began to come into my awareness that to come back to God often takes a struggle; a battle; a surrender. I decided that I was out of alignment in many of the things I was responsible for in my role as the CEO of my business. To the public, they saw this successful woman owning her own business with employees, loving life, and accomplishing big goals. But, deep down I was uneasy, frustrated, and feeling discontented from my day to day work. Behind the scenes I was drinking away my stress yet trying to hold on to any form of spiritual inspiration that I could (except for the Bible). I dabbled in new age, tarot cards, astrology, and anything that I thought would help me find my way back to me.

I had taught myself that being successful was a way to feel like I was worth something. Deep down I battled, *"The only way to fit in and be of value is to be smart and make a lot of money."* With this mantra playing in my head what did I do in this moment of 2013? I looked at additional work benchmarks to fulfill that uneasy need trying to get my attention. I thought I needed *MORE* work success, so I decided to make a commitment! *"Burn the boat!"* as they say and go all in!

I signed up for an intensive Executive Coaching certification program taught by a Harvard MBA mastermind, and stroked the check to an editor to get my business book completed by September of that year. I committed: I would do more speaking events, I would do more interviews, I would write more business articles, I would do more webinars, and I would create more technology solutions.

*Nothing was going to hold me back! This was going to give me the life I wanted. This was going to make my life fulfilled!* Ha! The stories we tell ourselves to give CPR to our soul; only to self-medicate with things to ignore what our true calling is.

You might say, *"Tricia what are you talking about? What you are telling me sounds pretty awesome. You were taking the steps to grow your career! What could be wrong with that?"*

Nothing actually, except for the signs that this wasn't my greatest path to fulfillment and healing.

I remember and will never forget it, the day, of the 2007 Virginia Tech shooting. I had been raised in Blacksburg, Virginia most of my childhood and had lived there during my college years, so Virginia Tech was close to my heart. I had so many memories of growing up, from looking for fishing worms on the drill field with my dad after a hard rain, to studying at the library while in high school to feel grown up and anchor the feeling of achievement, to the many not so great memories…

The day of the shooting struck my heart as I thought about the town's people that were not the college students, but the mothers and fathers, the business owners, the retired folks, and those who made up the tapestry of this town and treated the college students like extended family. I could feel the pain that day coming from the hearts of the people living there and all over the country.

I remember being on the back patio wearing my Virginia Tech sweatshirt when the phone rang, it was my sister. She told me that her son had been arrested in an FBI sting in Florida. I was in complete shock for a moment and then snapped out of it realizing that she was totally devastated.

I remember calling my mom that day to discuss his arrest and the talk turned to her denial of the dysfunction and abuse in our family but in the same sentence talking about our family sexual addictions and abuse. This all infuriated me. The shame and the denial was so heavy that I probably drank a lot that day just to push through it.

After a few weeks I remember my sister calling me and saying that her son's trial was coming up and she would need to go to Orlando. She didn't know if she could do it all on her own as her husband didn't want to go. I knew in the moment she told me, that I would drop everything and go with her. Just a few years earlier I had gone with her to Virginia when he tried to commit suicide, once again I would be there to help her through.

Karen and I ended up making flight arrangements for the trip together to Orlando. While we traveled, we talked about many things, but most prominent, the abuse that she experienced from my father

*My first plane trip at the age of seven, going to Michigan. My sister Regina attempted suicide.*

and how she had done everything in her power to break the cycle of abuse in her own family, yet for reasons she couldn't explain, this theme just kept arising. I listened to her, but also covered myself in denial. It had been easier to admit that the abuse only happened to her and by the time I was old enough, my father had changed. I had put the security blanket around me choosing to not acknowledge the times of depression he had, the few times he was in the mental hospital and the times where he drove the car at eighty miles an hour screaming at my mom while I was in the back seat scared out of my mind. Years later it would come to the surface of my awareness, things that I never even had remembered happening.

As we sat in the car together later that evening, tears began to stream down her face, *"I tried!"* she cried. *"I tried to make sure that abuse like this would not raise its head anymore. After everything I've lived through and yet still, here we are! I keep asking myself what did I do wrong? Why couldn't I stop this? Where did I go wrong?"*

It was then, in that moment of her criticizing herself emotionally, that I spoke. *"Karen, this is not your fault. The abuse that you endured is not your fault! You have to stop being the martyr. You are always trying to protect others, you are always trying to keep people safe while taking the punishment yourself. It's destroying you; you have got to stop."*

You see, all these years, she had never wanted anyone to know what she had gone through, but I knew. She had told me the things she had experienced before I was ever even born; she had shared a truth with me that before our mother had gotten pregnant with me, she had contemplated suicide.

She had said she felt like she couldn't live in the environment she was forced to live within anymore, but that I was her gift from God, her angel, to help her to continue living. She said it was proven to her as I had been brought home on Christmas day in 1970.

I never knew the full realization of her depression until the spring of 2015, when I found out she had attempted suicide again after I was born, as did my other sister. Being told I have a big calling and identifying early in my life my being called to be the rescuer, healer, fixer if you will, was a lot for one young girl to carry.

The truth of my father's abuse and even the abuse he had gone through himself as a child was always there but hidden just under the surface. There was always an extra seat at the table of every family function waiting for the shame and lies to arrive, for the elephant in the room to once again join us. This entity arrived often, called by the name of **SHAME**, it was just as much a part of our family as any physical person.

Sure, we tried not to let Shame live in our lives and be a part of our world, but no matter what, Shame always knew how to be one of the popular guests in the midst of any family situation. No matter how hard we tried to ignore it, there was no way out. Every corner we would turn, shame would come face to face with us, wanting attention and wanting to steal any hope of normalcy away from our family.

That night with Karen in the car in Orlando, Shame decided to take a place with us, in the back seat, along for the horrendous ride we would be taking the next morning to the courthouse. Thankfully though, another occupant was in the car through all of this, there was a heavenly Spirit ever present, helping us through these unchartered waters.

The following morning we used the GPS following the directions to the location but were uncertain where to park the car. The only place I could find was a parking garage that required quarters to be deposited every two hours. Fortunately, I had change in my wallet and we were able to take care of the meter.

I will never forget that moment, walking down the sidewalk as we headed to the courthouse that stood massively in front of us. I walked with my arm around Karen to give her whatever support I could, I felt every bit of her body shaking as she tried to hold her composure. What could I say? There were no words.

Walking through those big heavy doors, going through the metal detectors and finding a place to sit while waiting for the judgment that was to be given that day, created an energy that is hard to describe even to this day. Looking back, I realize I had a strength that was put upon me emotionally that could have only come from God. And I know today, God was with us every second.

I was given the right words, the connection, and the love to help Karen while we were waiting for the trial to begin. We sat in the coffee break room and chatted about everything and about nothing. I can't even remember. As time passed, I realized it was time to go back to the parking deck and put more quarters in the meter. I told Karen to stay inside so she didn't have to turn her cell phone back in (the attorney had approved her to keep it with her) and go through the metal detectors again. I didn't want to put her through anything more than what she already was going through.

Exiting the courthouse, I became extremely aware of my surroundings, I was in the middle of downtown Orlando next to the police station and the homeless shelter. I had no purse as I walked down the street to where I had parked my car; all I carried within my hands was my wallet (easily visible to anyone if they desired to look closely enough). Suddenly, I was able to feel the certainty of the pain and fear which was engulfing my sister and in turn engulfing me. I became aware of my vulnerability in this part of town with a wallet and all by myself, there was a fear within me, a feeling of insecurity.

Then in beat to the steps of my feet hitting the pavement, a set of words came to me.

> *Walk in faith.*
> *Do not forget.*
> *How strong you are.*
> *Walk in faith.*
> *Do not forget.*
> *How strong you are.*

Was I in a creative space in the moment? Not in the least. Yet these words came to my heart and mind with a beat of significance, I just didn't know what.

After placing coins into the meter, I headed back to the courthouse with confidence. As I found my sister and sat down beside her, I looked at her and said, *"A song just came to my mind, maybe we are supposed to write it together."* Even though it appeared that she was half listening to me, a compelling feeling urged me on.

I changed the subject and started talking about the book that I had with me called *Discover Your Strengths*, by Marcus Buckingham. We sat together and talked about how we are born and how we grow, contemplating on whether we become more of who we are or do we lose ourselves along the way, in the knowing of our gifts, strengths and talents.

It helped the time pass and before we knew it, we were called into the courtroom. We sat on the right side of the room behind her son, who was to be seated next to his attorney. I thought she was going to disintegrate when she saw him walk into the room in his orange jumpsuit, with handcuffs and chains shackled upon his arms and feet.

I have no idea how long we were in that courtroom that day; I can't recap what all was said, yet the memory that will always be forever in my mind was when my sister walked down the aisle and stood in front of the judge sharing her pain and crying over all of *this* that had become a reality. She sobbed over his life that would never be the same, how his goals of becoming a Chiropractor, a husband, and a citizen without a prison record was now a dream buried. I watched her grieve over the dreams of what she had hoped and fought for him to be.

Late that afternoon and into the evening we walked along the trail and pond next to our hotel. We went to dinner, ate chocolate, a lot of chocolate. Even though we knew what the day had held and what the next few years would look like, there was a level of comfort in knowing some of the certainty of the situation. It was what it was and, there was not much that could be done.

The next day we headed back to North Carolina to put things behind us and move on like we always had…never to talk about it much, as we allowed Shame and its counterpart named Secrecy, to once again become a normal part of our lives.

In that process for me, something within had been unlocked. Those words, *"WALK IN FAITH"* kept haunting me, as a melody started to play in my mind. Eventually, words began to form lyrics from somewhere within me or from a source that I can't explain. I wrote the words down in my journal as they marinated; it wasn't like I was a songwriter (God had given me this Warrior gift and here I was in complete denial).

Sure, I had written little songs for my son when he was born and whenever we were driving in the car to and from day care. But to say that it was a prominent part of my life would not be even close to accurate.

That next week after the trial, I headed to Albuquerque, New Mexico for a women's conference that I had signed up for a month earlier. I wasn't going to further my business but to dedicate time to myself and to my spirit. I went alone and looked forward to what the week would bring.

I remember the first day of the conference and the theme of *"Let your spirit soar."* The words that were shared spoke to me on a level deep within; so much so that I left the classes throughout the day and took several long baths. I was processing something within me, unlocking a deep part of my spirit that I hadn't felt before. There were times that I had picked myself up after a terrible loss (like during the loss of my first marriage and my miscarriage) but this was different. It was like the words from the Marcus Buckingham book were coding into my DNA mixing with this spirit that had been laid upon my heart.

That caused the words I had written for my dear sister to develop even deeper. Suddenly, as I sat within the sessions, I would realize I needed to get out my journal and write down new lyrics. It was as if a wave of needing to fulfill a requirement came over me (like a thirsty animal drinking from a trough). Still as the days went on, it had not been satisfied. I was literally consumed with the emotions of this song as the melody would play continuously in my head, the lyrics filling in around it. I found myself lost. Something larger than myself driving the process. I know now it was God that was bringing this to me.

When I got home from the conference, I shared the song with my husband. He was incredibly supportive of what I had written. Over the next few months songs started pouring out of me and before I knew it, I had written five songs by the second week of September. Music was consuming me like a river washing over a rock in a stream after a rainstorm. This passionate feeling called to me to see if any concerts were coming up that we could go to in the area.

I saw that Martina McBride was going to be playing in Charlotte and I instantly became excited. She was one of my absolute favorite artists and I knew most, if not all of her songs by heart. We decided to get seats as close as possible to the stage, we ended up being so close in row seventeen.

The excitement of the concert gave me inspiration. I thought, *"How cool would it be to get my songs into the hands of Martina McBride?"* With this inner voice speaking to me, I went to a local music guy who had basic recording tools and sang my songs acapella into his microphone. He burned these songs into a plain silver CD and gave it to me. I was so proud of those songs even though there was no music to accompany them. In reflection, it felt like a dream realizing that these words had come out of me from somewhere I didn't even know had existed within my soul.

A few days later we headed to the concert. I had my CD with me and had no idea how I was going to get it to her. We had no backstage passes, we had no VIP seating, all we had were normal seats…but that didn't stop me from wanting to accomplish my main goal. Now you might be curious to know what my goal was, my goal was finding a way to get my CD into Martina McBride's hands, even though I had no connections or an easy way to do so.

The concert started with an opening band, I honestly can't even remember who it was as I was fixated on getting my little CD into her hands. It was what I felt I needed to do, a risk I needed to take. I maneuvered myself all the way down to the front row, there was a group of women there having fun, in my excitement and with every burst of courage I had, I turned to them and said, *"These are my own original songs and I feel like I am to get them to Martina McBride."* They instantly adopted me in and said, *"Stay here with us and we'll help you!"*

Security however, had a mission and mind of their own. They realized I did not have front row seats (ha-ha!) so they asked me to go back to my seat, watching me closely. Isn't it interesting how something can push you through a fear and cause you to act quickly? I had been there for several minutes but couldn't find the right *"timing"* to toss the CD on stage. Once security realized I hadn't left and was not officially seated there, they once again approached to send me go back to my seat. I knew it was now or never! Instantly I got up the courage to quickly reach out and slide my CD across the stage toward Martina McBride.

In seconds I was heading back to my seat (luckily, they didn't kick me out of the concert!) and I heard her say into the microphone. *"A CD, thank you."*

It was in that moment that I realized that my goal had become a reality.

That feeling of accomplishment gave me momentum, driving me to complete more songs, and record an album. During that recording process I wrote a song which opened up the opportunity for me to sing at the Keller Williams Realty convention to over 7,000 attendees.

The hidden Warrior in me arose again in December of 2010 at a *Date with Destiny* event with Tony Robbins. I didn't know all that would lay ahead for me, I was definitely ready for what would be revealed, I went all in and focused on doing the work totally at this event!

On the second day, Tony Robbins asked a question and I was one of the two thousand in the room who raised their hand. However, something caused him to pick me to speak to and give my insight. Somehow, all the pieces of the pain that had been locked inside me for so long came forth in my words, I said to him, *"I am here to get my breakthrough."*

"*Come out to the aisle here beside me,*" he responded.

I can't explain all the things that happened in that encounter except I can share that two part of me, 'Scared Girl' and 'Unstoppable' came to the surface. What I do know is that at the end of the process I broke out in song with the microphone in my hand and sang clearly. The whole room was at an energy level I had never in my life experienced, but at the same time I knew it was who I was. What I was doing in that moment was my calling! I remember finishing the song as he said to me, "*And who is this person in front of me?*"

"*This is the real Tricia.*" I responded with a mix of smile and tears on my face.

He then asked me something so profound. "*Tricia, when you write your songs, do they come from the pain that you have experienced?*" I responded. "*Yes.*"

Smiling at me he responded, "*That is the gift in the pain.*" I will never forget that moment, as he looked at me and he sang to me the words of a song by Bruno Mars, "*cause your amazing just the way you are....*"

When he was done working with me, I began walking towards the back to go to the restroom in a surreal state, knowing the REAL ME was present in that moment. I turned to walk toward the back and there was a line of hundreds upon hundreds of people that were waiting to talk to me and hug me. One after another, people began to speak to me, "*You gave me my breakthrough.*"

"*You said my story*"

"*Thank you*"

"*I now feel like I can do it…*"

All week-long, people came to me saying things like, *"You have changed my life"*, *"I will see you on Oprah"* and so much more. Weeks later, I received a letter from a young woman who had been at the event, she shared with me that because I shared my story, she had committed to never contemplating suicide again.

Over the years I have received countless stories from those that my story inspired, saying now they realized they could achieve something in their life that they never thought possible.

### The Warrior Weapon

What I have come to understand is God was knocking on my heart to awaken me and to give me the spiritual gifts that he had put inside of me from the moment I was born.

That conference with Tony Robbins showed me that I knew that my life work had to involve sharing my VOICE through singing, writing, and even through art. At the event while my eyes where closed, I saw myself as a three year old little girl swinging on a swing; singing and writing songs while knowing they were to bring healing: *It was who I was made to be.* (In 2015 I had this vision under the Holy Spirit again. That inner three year old's name was 'Brightness.')

It has been continuously reaffirmed to me that God's Ordained purpose for my life is to evangelize, share healing, connections, love, and encouragement through the gifts of song, writings, and teaching in front of people. I want them to explore God and know God.

*My inner warrior shinning through*

This is why unlocking my inner warrior has been a long journey; a continuous process. I am going to be completely transparent with you. To become a Warrior, it takes the willingness to listen to your heart and be open to traveling an often-uncertain path that many make think is lofty. Even still, I want to encourage you to be open to the process of where God may be leading you. It is a serious and important endeavor.

God has a plan for you that you may not be able to see all of the pieces yet, but you have to trust Him. Let these stories within this book challenge you, awaken you, and open your heart and mind to unlocking the warrior that is there; deep inside you.

In high school I had been told by my teacher that my voice wasn't as good as others. That made me close off any possibility of using my voice in my career; I believed another's opinion and a statement that someone else told me. I chose to believe one person's opinion of me, to the point I almost lost my entire voice, even though others would tell me I was gifted. The enemy wanted to strangle me to a whisper and silence my truth and gifts.

People will come across your path and they will either speak life into you or they will speak death into you.

BUT GOD…. has equipped you as a Warrior to rise up and be the person he created you to be.

*"Arise, shine, for your light has come, and the glory of the Lord rises upon you. See, darkness covers the earth and thick darkness is over the peoples, but the Lord rises upon you and his glory appears over you. Nations will come to your light, and kings to the brightness of your dawn.*

> *Lift up your eyes and look about you: All assemble and come to you; your sons come from afar, and your daughters are carried on the hip. Then you will look and be radiant, your heart will throb and swell with joy; the wealth on the seas will be brought to you, to you the riches of the nations will come."*
> Isaiah 60:1-5

That day in 2014 at Hilton Head changed the course of my life, once I dedicated all the pieces of myself to Him, things began to change. In August of 2015 at the John Maxwell conference John had an optional worship service. At the worship service John shared, *"If you have ever felt you didn't have the father you needed or you were without a father, God wants you to know right now that HE IS YOUR REAL FATHER."* I began to cry and in the alter call my husband rose and gave his heart to the Lord. We stood side by side hugging and crying knowing that God was going to be the center of all we would do.

Every single thing I do is for HIS GLORY. I <u>*choose*</u> to let my voice be heard.

Whether writing, singing, speaking, coaching, teaching, or creating a story through art, I know that these are the tools for me to evangelize what God has done in my life and be a testament of what He can do in yours.

Rise Up Warrior. It is your time.

Lyrics to *Rise Up* and *Walk In Faith* are located in the last chapter.

## STRATEGIES TO UNLOCK YOUR INNER WARRIOR

1. What is something someone told you about a talent or a natural strength you might have had growing up that you realize made you stop doing it or throw it away?

_____
_____
_____
_____
_____

2. How much you willing to challenge the things you believe about yourself and rewrite the story of your life? Begin to rewrite your story, from your truth, your heart.

_____
_____
_____
_____
_____

3. What pain in your life have you run from and what opportunity could you have that uses the pain in your heart for something transformational?

_____
_____
_____
_____
_____

4. In committing to reading this book, what are some lies the enemy is telling you that you KNOW you have to take captive and declare them as lies?

_____

_____

_____

_____

5. Go to the internet and do a search on *"Your identity in Christ scripture."* Find 3 Bible Scriptures that support why you were created, what calling He has for you, and what Spirit has He put inside of you.

Read these scripture often, get them into your Spirit, believe them, live them!

Rewrite them into affirmation statements. For example, *"I am strong and courageous."*

State these everyday to allow the Holy Spirit to work this into your mindset and your daily living.

# CHAPTER 2
# THE WARRIOR BATTLE
By Tricia Andreassen

It was January 14, 2018 when secrets of brokenness in my family lines would come to the surface for all the world to see.

Laying in bed with a headache I heard my cell phone messenger alert from my cousin, showing that her sister had just been arrested for horrifically abusing their thirteen children and holding them captive.

My favorite childhood cousin on my mom's side of the family, Louise Turpin, had been taken into custody along with her husband David. Growing up just a year and a half apart in age we spent many weekends going to the mall together, playing board games, sitting on her Grandma's (my favorite Aunt and my mom's sister) red cement patio laughing and playing hand-clapping games. *"Miss Mary Mack, Mack, Mack… all Dressed in Black…Black…Black… with Silver Buttons, Buttons, Buttons all down her back. She asked her mother for fifty cents, to see the Elephants climb the fence."* We would try and go as fast as possible without messing up.

This was one of my childhood best friends where we would talk about who we had crushes on and what our dreams were. How had this happened? I had known about the abuse on my dad's side of the family but to see a family member from my mom's side hit International News was…. well…. Numbing.

Louise and I were close. Her parents were married and lived down the road where every once and a while we would visit, oddly the energy in the house never felt comforting to me. I could tell that Louise's parents didn't get along, so most times we spent together were at her grandma's where we would eat Bundt cake, have contests to see who could blow the biggest bubbles and come Fall make the largest pile of leaves possible so we could run and jump in them. It was these memories that helped keep me sane from all the other things in my life that I wanted to escape from. And now I imagine it was the same feeling for her.

When the news hit, my email as well as text messages started going off like crazy, feelings of my childhood I wanted to forget came flooding into my mind. Louise's sister Elizabeth had connected a few years prior with me on Facebook and when my Aunt Louise passed away in 2011, I decided to attend the funeral. Although I was not a fan to go back to Princeton I felt called to go because my Aunt Louise and I were very close, and I loved her dearly. My mom and dad were not able to travel, and I wanted to also go on their behalf. When I arrived, I had hoped to see Louise because I missed her and had not seen her physically in years. We had had conversations on Facebook talking about our children and basic small talk about our memories growing up, but I was told she was unable to come. I figured it was due to being such a long trip and having the responsibility of being a mom.

*My Aunt Louise who was so special to me*

Before heading to the hotel to get settled in for the next day's service, I decided to stop by and see my Aunt's house that had held so many memories and visit with my cousin Phyllis, the mom of Louise and Elizabeth. Walking into the home that was once beautifully kept and adorned, I was shocked to find it in shambles and filthy. It was so hard to walk into. I knew Phyllis had battled many issues and my Aunt did her best to take care of her but once my Aunt was in a nursing-home, I assume that her home started falling away.

My son Jordan who was only in 6th grade at the time gave me a look like, *"Mom, where in the world are we?"* Our luxury home in a waterfront community along the shores of Lake Norman compared to this was the perfect example of two different worlds. I had always felt out of my element in West Virginia. When I was a kid, we had a piece of property with a trailer on it that we would go to on the weekends as my mom Pastored a church in a nearby town called Athens. Perhaps I should just be direct for anyone reading this. I don't mean this to sound terrible, but some would tell me that I always acted older than my age and carried myself differently than others, like I was better than them. The truth was I was living out the books that had been placed in my hands at a young age. I remember being as young as seven years old and reading the book on our book shelf, *"The Magic of Thinking Big."* My older sister Karen had me reading Dale Carnegie as early as age thirteen so I guess you could say I was putting into practice what I was reading.

> *"As a man thinketh in his heart…."*
> Proverbs 23:7

From that environment in West Virginia I had made a clear decision. I was going to do whatever I could to be successful in business, to break out of any mold that other family members might be living. I made that decision as young as sixteen, entering my Senior year of High School. I gave up singing to be in the Deca Club and get my first job with Hallmark Cards.

Going back to the funeral of my Aunt Louise (my cousin Louise was named after her) brought a wave of emotions. I struggled even with the drive going there. My husband was traveling for work but I was able to take my son for company which was a tremendous blessing. I felt like I was stepping back in time to the remnants of my childhood that I had wanted to leave behind. In fact, I felt grateful that I had broken the life cycle of everything I had escaped. It wasn't until I arrived at the funeral home that it became more evident that I still hadn't let go of the pain and anger that I had pushed down so deeply.

I was in the funeral home during the viewing, before the actual service began and my Uncle John walked in holding his cane. Although very old, the little girl within me came forward. It was a combination of that little girl and the angry teenager that wanted to fight but didn't know how. She emerged from behind the strong business woman and CEO that I had become. Every part of my insides began to shake and my mind began to scream into my spirit, *"Get out now!"* I knew in an instant there was no way I could share the room with this man. The ex-husband of my Aunt, the Grandfather of my cousins, and my Uncle. He made my skin crawl and I detested the thought of having to be near him. I knew the evil, sick man that had fondled my body, had forced his tongue down my throat and would be allowed to drive me in the car by myself at a very young age while putting his hand on my knee. The memories of him made me sick.

Fervently I went to find my son who was outside in the lounge area.

I said, *"Let's go."*

*"The service is over?"*

*"No,"* I responded. *"But we are leaving."*

On the way home I told him that was the Uncle who had hurt me. I had a talk with him when he was just in 3rd grade about how someone could be inappropriate and it might not be a stranger. I was honest with him and created the communication about this topic as I knew communication was key in explaining to my son what types of abuse existed in this world. You might say that he was too young for that, but I am grateful that he has grown to be a compassionate leader helping many young people, I am greatly proud of him. On the drive home from West Virginia to North Carolina I knew I never wanted to visit Princeton, West Virginia ever again. EVER. All that it held for me was memories I wanted to forget… Real…Raw…Trauma.

I had done a pretty good job at closing those doors. Talking to my cousins Elizabeth and Louise was easy on Facebook. Louise and I would share stories about growing up and the games we would play. She would share pictures of the kids and when she told me she was expecting again in her forty's I was amazed because I was just a bit younger than her. I never questioned it as she seemed happy and they had been married for such a long time.

I never thought much of Louise not coming home much because I felt I could relate to her desire of not wanting to return to West Virginia. We shared that sentiment of wanting to leave and never come back. I am not talking about the town itself as much as the memories it most likely held for both of us. My research showed that my grandparents and great grandparents and generational downline originated from this area. As an overcomer; a Warrior, I don't feel this way now, but, back then, when she told me that she was marrying David and would move away, my response was more of, *"Good for you!"* We both had talked about moving away someday, I knew I had wanted to get away from the life I had lived growing up and reinvent myself. So, I understood what she was doing.

After my Aunt's funeral I went back to my *"successful"* life and shut the door on that past.

When the news hit about my cousin Louise Turpin and the *"House of Horrors"* case, my mind went directly to the children. I thought of what my sister had shared in her physical abuse from my dad. I thought of what I had gone through. It rocked me to the core because it was exposing family SHAME once again, front and center this time. Again, the question came into my mind, *"How could these cycles be repeated over and over?"* The answer that the Holy Spirit gave me is one that would be difficult for me to share but from what I know about my dad being abused as a child and the things I have come to find out about David Turpin has given me great insight (and distress that only I can take to God in prayer). I do know that there is a common thread. I only share things when God calls me to so at this time, I will table this part of the story.

Just months before the news broke, I have been prompted by the Holy Spirit to read about Satanic Ritual Abuse. Little did I know that the Lord was giving me a glimpse into what could have been going on behind closed doors. As I traveled with Elizabeth to visit Louise in jail, I began to ask Elizabeth if she knew if Louise had been involved in any forms of ritual work. It was then that she told me about Louise using the Ouija Board to ask questions. I was told she practiced in witchcraft that involved spells and putting blood in the actual spell as well as having voodoo dolls to place a spell on her husband. I was told that one spell had scared Louise so terribly that she had thrown away the voodoo doll; indicating it has turned David's eyes completely black.

My research continued to expand on this topic because I knew I had been called to be an Unstoppable Warrior for Christ under the scripture of Ephesians 6:10-18.

*"Finally, be strong in the Lord and in his mighty power. Put on the full armor of God, so that you can take your stand against the devil's schemes. For our struggle is not against flesh and blood, but against the rulers, against the authorities, against the powers of this dark world and against the spiritual forces of evil in the heavenly realms. Therefore, put on the full armor of God, so that when the day of evil comes, you may be able to stand your ground, and after you have done everything, to stand. Stand firm then, with the belt of truth buckled around your waist, with the breastplate of righteousness in place, and with your feet fitted with the readiness that comes from the gospel of*

*peace. In addition to all this, take up the shield of faith, with which you can extinguish all the flaming arrows of the evil one. Take the helmet of salvation and the sword of the Spirit, which is the word of God. And pray in the Spirit on all occasions with all kinds of prayers and requests."*

I saw Louise three times during the first half of the year. When we met, she asked me to be the Power of Attorney for her finances. She wanted me to put the house up for sale and help with filing taxes and other business details as she knew my experience in real estate and business. I declined, although I had many that wanted me to do it all, gain access to the house for money, etc. I stood firm in not doing so. Those conversations where bizarre and although I can't prove it, I do believe that there were Satanic Practices going on under this household. I spent hours researching the background of photos, dissecting items in the house such as the comic books on display and what they were about as well as the crystal balls on the mantel.

I feel God gave me this Warrior Revelation as it was confirmed on a plane trip after visiting with Louise, on the flight home a Pastor happened to sit right beside me. He was not supposed to be sitting there next to me, somehow, he and his wife had been separated on the flight. There was an open seat for him to join her after taking off, but he told the flight attendant he was going to stay where he was, sitting next to me. As we began to talk it was revealed how God was using him to teach me. He shared that he had a calling in working with SRA (Satanic Ritual Abuse) survivors. Up until that time I didn't know what SRA meant, but he told me to begin to study the ministry of Kay Holman and her personal work in this field.

During this time, videos where released on one of Louise's daughters singing her own songs on YouTube. I thought back to those times I did that as I have shared with you in this book. Music and words were a way for this beautiful young girl to get her through the pain.

My heart calls to her heart all the time. I guess that is a reaffirmation of why I have a passion to help people discover the voice that God wants them to use. I remember someone saying, *"Tricia! You told me to use my voice and I am now!"* She proceeded to use a voice and word that I am sure broke God's heart. You always know the voice God is calling to you to use, just continue to seek Him.

## Slaying the Giant

One morning I talked with the Dr. Oz producer and they wanted to film a documentary in Princeton, West Virginia giving insight to the life of Louise. My cousin Elizabeth asked me if I would be by her side as I had been her coach and mentor for a while. I knew it was going to be difficult for me personally to go back. While the media and public had their eyes on the Turpin Case story, no one but my closest friends knew that I was in my own battle story.

*I said I didn't want to come back here and now I am coming back with a camera crew?* Elizabeth and I drove up to meet with the Dr. Oz team. Before going to the hotel, I wanted to go back to our weekend homeplace where our trailer had sat. It was a short trip from the Athens Church of God where I had done my first preaching event at the age of thirteen. Driving down the road my mind was filled with nostalgia and

*Where my Uncle molested me and the land that was turned into a junk yard*

a mix of feelings I couldn't describe. But when we drove down Hwy 19 and saw the land where I once lived, now a junk yard, my complete self crumbled inside. Elizabeth stayed in the car as I went to walk the property, an old metal frame of a car sat in ruins and trash was scattered all over the place. Seeing something in the distance that I couldn't make out I continued to walk closer to it, within moments I realized it was a dead carcass of a deer with its body on its side and the skin rotted off exposing the skull and the bones.

*Echols Trailer Park in Blacksburg, Virginia where I lived from Kindergarten to 4th grade*

Right then and there I began to sob, a sob so deep within me of things that I had wanted to forget for all those years and all that was left was gross, rotted, memories. I realized I had no homeplace of any kind left. The trailer park in Blacksburg now were condominiums. There was nothing from my childhood tangible in a way of a home to come back to; to see my roots.

I had no choice but to gather myself together for the filming. After all, the focus was on the International story. It brought such revelation to me about how many stories like mine are never told, how many stories never get heard so patterns are not repeated, and how many children that are getting looked over, ignored, and not cared for. My heart was so tender, that I did the most unexpected thing.

During the filming the crew wanted to take us by Elizabeth's grandfather's house. My heart ached for her as she was so distraught and in fear of facing him. I told the crew that if we were going to drive by, I wanted to confront him. They were wonderful and concerned for us, not wanting us to be in danger of any kind. I looked at them and said, *"Here's the thing, if you don't want me to go to his door then when you are done with this work drop me back off at the hotel and I will come over by myself. With or without you I am going. I am not going home with this on my shoulders, I must be unstoppable, an unstoppable warrior for those who don't have a voice."* I put my arms around Elizabeth whom I will always love and said, *"If you can't go, I will go and be the warrior for both of us."* We got in the car and proceeded to my Uncle's house.

As we drove by, he was walking in the front yard. Before we had a chance to pull around, he had gone inside of the house. Again, the crew said, *"Tricia, you don't have to do this,"* with my John Maxwell Leadership Bible in hand I said, *"Yes, I do."*

While walking up the sidewalk to his door I prayed that God would help me to do and say what I needed to say. In that moment a feeling of calmness came over me, I know Jesus was right there with me to face my abuser after all these years. The screen door was open, and he was sitting in an old recliner, I knocked on the door and he slowly got up and shuffled his way to the door.

No longer did I see the man I had known in my childhood years and what is even more supernatural is I didn't see the man like I had at the funeral just a few years prior. What I mean by this is I had seen him as this big, evil giant that I needed to be afraid of. With God inside me so fully now and standing as a Warrior, God gave me the vision to see the giant no more and see a small man who was just that…. a man.

I said, *"I don't know if you remember me, I am Carl and Shirley's daughter, Patty."* I then continued on with chit chat saying *"I was in the area and I needed to come and see you. I just needed to talk to you, I wanted to come and just ask you. I know you are up in age now; do you feel ready to meet Jesus after you pass on? Do you feel you have settled things with him?"*

He went into a speech about how he read his Bible everyday and that for years he was in ministry helping in funeral situations and such.

I continued forward in the conversation. *"That's good, I felt it was important to come see you because although you may not say anything,*

*I want you to know that I remember the things that were done to me and I needed to come see you personally and tell you that I forgive you. If there is anything you need to address with God, I want to remind you that you still have the opportunity."*

He deflected again asking about my parents and telling me how many grandchildren he had and how many great grandchildren he had. That he heard about Louise on the news and that was sad. He went on to say he went to my Aunt Louise's funeral, then he talked specifically with facts and details that I know were to show me that he was in his full mind. I also was given awareness that when I said *"I forgive you"* that he didn't respond with the opportunity that was given him to make things right with me and with God.

I said my goodbye's and left so calmly. When I got into the vehicle with Elizabeth and the filming team, they commented how calm the conversation seemed and how long it went on. All I know is that ONLY GOD could have put the spirit in me that I operated in. ONLY GOD could give me the heart-healing-words of forgiveness and mean them.

A few weeks later, my cousins and I decided to give a statement to the Princeton Police. This was one of the hardest things I ever had to do; explain the sexual abuse that had happened in writing and by recording. I left the courthouse that day and took the long way home through Blacksburg, Virginia where I was raised and to reflect where I had come from and what God had brought me through. I knew in those moments that my identity was not my possessions or remains on this earth. The work I was doing for God every waking moment would be my legacy.

After I arrived back in North Carolina I was informed that the Police decided to charge my Uncle with a Sex Crime. They told him to get his affairs in order and they would be back in a few days to formally charge him. Within a couple of days, he died in his home, even through he was in complete health. He was known to be alway working even at his age.

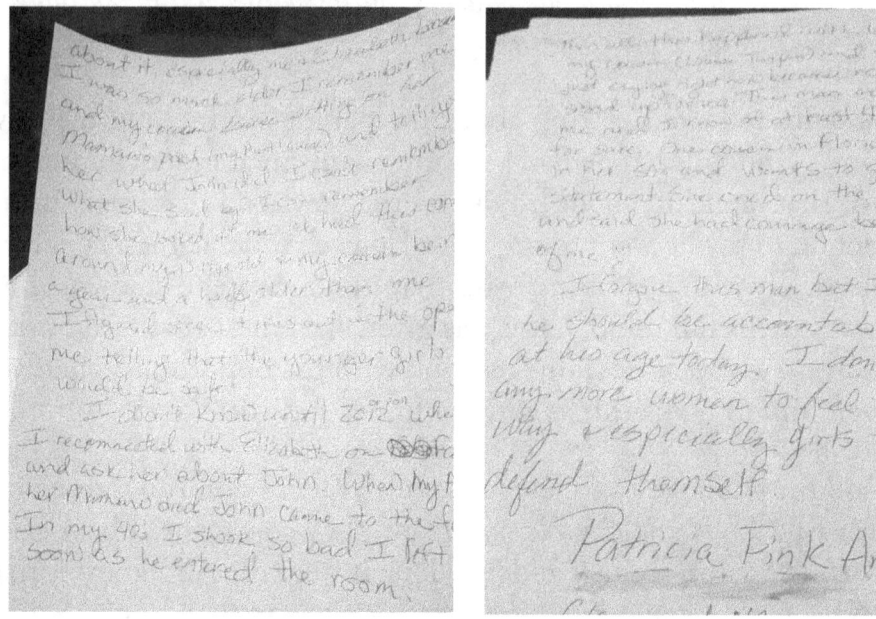
*Statement filed against my Uncle*

I am sharing this because you may be thinking that you aren't a warrior but I am here to tell you that when you can surrender your full life to Christ and let him be your leader, He will raise you up as a Warrior. With him you will be unstoppable when called for.

Carry On Warrior.

Hold Your Value.

Know You Are A Child Of The Most High King.

## STRATEGIES TO UNLOCK YOUR INNER WARRIOR

1. What is a secret in your past that you need to kneel down in prayer and give it over to God? He wants to carry your burdens and He wants you to come through the other side in freedom.

_____
_____
_____


2. What have you allowed the enemy to tell you to let secrets and shame hold you back to the person God wants you to see? He wants YOU to see how HE SEES YOU.

_____
_____
_____
_____


3. Did you have a relationship with SHAME? Yes, I have named it like a real person. Perhaps it's time to write that *"breakup"* letter. Find 3 Bible Scriptures that reveal how much the Lord God loves you. Write them out and go to the mirror and speak them into your heart.

_____
_____
_____
_____
_____

## JOURNAL/REFLECTIONS

# CHAPTER 3
# REACH BEYOND!
By Anna Brehm Anderson

When I agreed to be an Author in this book I thought it would be a straightforward topic to explore and write about! It would be simple!

Not in the slightest.

What surprised me is as I researched and began writing; I came to realize that my own life's map was just a guideline, and there have been many unexpected and intentional detours. We all experience inner struggles and triumphs of some kind during our time on earth. For most of us, we don't take the time to recognize what we have accomplished and too quickly move on to the next moment or dwell on the negative.

All those earlier lessons have molded me to be the person I am today and I wouldn't trade them for the world. My astonishment is all my accomplishments in life and what it took for me to recognize, develop and maintain my Inner Warrior.

For so many of us, life can be similar to the movement of a playground teeter-totter. For me, it's a perfect metaphor for my ups and downs in life. My imaginary teeter-totter has me on both ends and I am constantly adjusting my position to keep balanced. One minute I am on top of the world, happy, content, and my life's plan is right on target. The next moment I am at a low point, running away from my shadow, questioning my path.

In today's world it isn't difficult to become sidetracked from our dreams. We create the perfect plan and sometimes without fail someone or something disrupts the balance, scattering our thoughts and ideas in every direction. Creating our life's teeter-totter to be unbalanced.

The teeter-totter rests on the pivot point, the fulcrum, and is unmovable. This pivot point of my teeter-totter came to be known as my Inner Warrior! It is built on my core values, life's experiences, and spiritual beliefs. These qualities are what I rely on to maintain my life's balance in my everyday world.

The first time I encountered the Inner Warrior concept was during a period in my life where nothing seemed to be going smoothly. Personally, it was a very difficult time; I was experiencing self-doubt, anxiety, and deflated dreams. My professional career, though successful was a constant battleground of pettiness and negativity. That million-dollar question continued to seep into my thoughts, *"What is my purpose in life?" "What ideals am I holding on to?" "What actions need to be taken to strengthen my pivot point – my Inner Warrior?" "How do I find life's balance – my life's purpose?"*

A friend shared Herman Hesse's quote with me: *"Some of us think holding on makes us strong, but sometimes it's letting go."*

Sprinkled throughout this chapter are self-study activities. They may assist you in detecting actions, which are deterring you from achieving personal growth and balance. For me, the roadblocks I had created were minimized when I took ownership. One of my favorite truisms: Every day can be a *"New Beginning"* and every day is a *"New Opportunity!"* Don't focus on the failures of yesterday! There may even be times when a positive idea presents itself where you thought only negative resolutions were possible. Stay on your positive path of determination and take it one step at a time and through the teeter-totter concept, you may find a new view of yourself. Along with these concepts one may need the guidance of a trained professional who can help begin the process of understanding and how to take that first step towards positive change.

Using the following activity, I started my quest for balance. Stop everything!!! First, let's take time – right now to reflect. Yes, Now. Take five or ten minutes for this exercise! Reflect and Focus!

Close your eyes and take a deep breath, and concentrate on what makes you smile, lightens your heart, calms your soul, and provides balance? Repetition provides the practice to master something new. Training for a 5K run is very different than training for a marathon, but it all begins with creating a training program and then continuously repeating those steps.

If you don't have a positive routine in place – NOW is the time to create one! In the beginning it may be difficult to sit quiet and reflect, you may find yourself wondering *"What should I think about?"* If you have a routine in place, take some quiet time to review it.

**Let's pre-plan.** Locate a quiet area in your home; determine what the most comfortable sitting position is for you. It may be useful to jot down a few entries in your journal: quotes, prayers, poems, troublesome thoughts, and times you are thankful for. Hmmm, paper or electronic journaling - I recommend paper – you are less apt to look at your texts, check the weather, and emails, (I told you I have also been there before!) Begin practicing sitting still, quiet breaths, eyes closed can help you maintain that positive inner presence and focus. It may take several practice sessions just to get comfortable, begin with abbreviated bits of time. Again, sit quietly, gentle breathing, and focus. Don't be multi–tasking, checking emails, and viewing social media, then wonder why 10 minutes from now you are frustrated and feel a routine will never, ever work for you. I speak from experience. Have patience. We know ourselves. Don't begin making up excuses to stop the routine, to self-sabotage.

**Let's put what we practiced - in action.** It's the start of your day! Within the first 15 minutes you have set the tone not only for your attitude, but how your day is going to play out. Have you decided if it is going to be successful or are you going to sabotage it?

> *"Every day may not be good…*
> *but there is something good in every day."*
> Alice Morse Earle.

First, don't begin your day by tapping the snooze alarm, then lay there stressing over your reasons for lack of sleep or your mood! Make that CHOICE to get out of bed and know God will be with you every step of the way. Today is the day to start the transformation and become the warrior you want to be.

Sit Up! Place both feet firmly on the floor and Give Thanks! Be grateful that God made you.

**Let's begin!** Where was that quiet place in house? What is your favorite sitting position? Close your eyes, take a deep breath and focus. Keep trying; don't get discouraged. Start again and again if need be, it will become easier. You will soon see how the fragile inner you is growing stronger. With a clear vision – this activity can lead you to a positive start to your day.

It has been proven when we begin the day with a positive attitude it will carry through the day. This doesn't mean issues can't crop up for you personally, in family or in your career relationships, but with introducing meditation to your day, your Inner Warrior will be more apt to handle those situations.

It is through the practice of meditation and journaling that I have learned to peel away the layers of anxiety and challenge myself to confront change and take responsibility for myself. Will Smith said it so eloquently, *"When you take responsibility, you now have the power to change, take control, and create a better life. It really doesn't matter whose fault it is that something is broken. It's your responsibility to fix it!"* It took many attempts for ME to take that first step and break the cycle, but I have. My Inner Warrior was discovered and grew more confident.

The process of defining and strengthening my Inner Warrior started by investigating how a warrior is depicted in Medieval History. The illustrations I encountered portrayed a powerful, confident person; face flushed with determination, holding a shield in one hand, a sword in the other hand, waging war against who they believe to be their enemy.

Their battles were fought over land boundaries, family safety, freedom of speech, and religion. Can this be the same image and principles of a present day warrior? We may use different weapons in today's contemporary world, but our causes are somewhat the same. We need to protect ourselves, our family, defend our freedom and religious beliefs, and be a caregiver of mankind.

So if past and present day warriors are similar in causes do they have like characteristics? Today many of us still convey the same determination, strength of body, mind and soul, bravery, and integrity in our everyday life. This revelation made me curious, do I project these attributes in my daily routine, and is this truly how I see myself and who I am?

To understand my moods and emotional pattern, I inserted my modern day life into History's portrait of a warrior.

- **My Battle is everyday life.** In order to mature and improve my behavior I must know what my purpose in life is. Where do I want to be today, tomorrow, next week, or in 5 years? Where will I provide positive impact, serve mankind, and be the person God created me to be? By continuously asking myself; *"What role does God want me to play in this world,"* my life's purpose will continue to evolve.

My Inner Warrior is the person who fights everyone else's battles but my own. Maybe, just maybe it's easier to fight their battles than to face my own. I fear the unknown, the world of *"what if's!"* My Inner Warrior sometimes diminishes the positive goals I have set making me feel inferior. Thoughts creep in *"Do you really think you will be promoted"* or, *"That idea isn't going to be accepted..."*

I am a woman, an author, an entrepreneur, a wife, a mother, a grandmother, a great-grandmother, a friend, and a co-worker. With so many social roles isn't it surprising my life gets overwhelming and my teeter-totter unbalanced? Let's face it – some days my life isn't what I had envisioned, but those are the days I have learned to dig deeper and to understand what it takes to bring happiness, success, and balance into my life. There are many ways to challenge and win a battle, conquer an enemy, but you need to take that very first step. When I am fighting the internal war, I know I need to move past that fierce outwardly persona and find within me the strength to understand and fight this particular battle. What is your battle?

- **My facial expression of determination is fear**. I am afraid of failing, of walking away from my goals, of being different.

*"You don't fear change. You fear the unknown. If you knew the future would be great, you'd welcome the change to get there. Well, the future IS great. Proceed."*
Joe Vitale

I have come to realize, scars make great stories, but I can't let them define whom I am. Many of us try to *"hide"* our inner challenges by acting out via the outer warrior. I found, the outside world is able to distinguish which scenario I'm experiencing based on my body language, my tone of voice, facial expressions. Can you recognize when your outer warrior is masquerading as someone else to hide problems or insecurities? Who are you seeking approval from?

- **My enemy doesn't have a face.** More often than not my enemy is ME. My enemy can be ego, impatience, laziness, unrealistic demands on others and myself. From living in the past to the fear of moving forward. My negative warrior could manifest an impenetrable shield to protect me when I was discouraged, feeling powerless and afraid, or fighting some other internal battle. In this early discovery period, I wrapped myself in an invisible shield, protecting myself. Later I learned the shield was pushing away the very people who loved me and could help me. Do you know what your enemy looks like? Could you be fighting the wrong enemy?

To triumph over my enemy, I surrendered control to God. There is not an area in my life that God is not willing to help me. I realized God will guide my steps; nothing is too trivial.

> *"Trust in the Lord with all your heart; do not depend on your own understanding. Seek his will in all you do, and he will show you which path to take."*
> Proverbs 3:5-6

My shield and sword are not made of metal but have been forged by my faith and trust in God. His armor protects me!

- **My shield is faith.** As I grow in faith, my confidence in God grows.

> *"Now faith is being sure of what we hope for and certain of what we do not see."*
> Hebrews 11:1

- **My sword is truth.** It is my trust in God! Many times we trust others more than we trust ourselves. As soldiers in God's army, it is our responsibility and duty to use His Word to discern the truth and then follow it.

> *"When God's Word shows us something wrong in ourselves, we can use this spiritual weapon to "surgically" remove the offending thoughts and actions."*
> 2 Corinthians 10:4-5

I visualize the shield and sword symbols to remind me a warrior knows they must build their spiritual confidence in order to overcome challenges in life. It has taken me many years to understand and unlock my Inner Warrior. Through meditation, prayer, and mindfulness, I am mentally, physically, and spiritually prepared to take on not only the challenges that enter into my life, but also to celebrate the positive accomplishments.

Are your values the same as the ones you grew up with or have you adopted others based on maturity or because of peer pressure?

Do you recognize what steps you need to take to unify your Inner Warrior and to maintain a balanced teeter-totter?

For many of us, we don't realize how social media changes our moods, our focus, and views on the world. We allow ourselves to be inundated with other people's triumphs and setbacks. We get sidetracked from our own goals and intentions by focusing on theirs, creating an unbalanced teeter-totter.

Have you ever begun the day in an *"OK"* type of mood and then after reading posts on social media your mood has changed? You discover you are irritated, jealous, and judgmental all because of a post that took you twenty seconds to read? Most of the time the full story, isn't even being told and yet these posts rock our teeter-totter. It is only natural to offer kudos for someone's good news and provide encouragement during his or her setbacks, but being connected continuously to society, has drawbacks.

As a child of the '50's and well into my mid '40's, I received my *"news and updates"* via a family member, friend, radio, television, or the newspaper. But with the introduction of the Internet, a never-ending stream of excess data is being released and consumed. So it is not a surprise that a person's focus is derailed and we have difficulty maintaining our positive balance. Yet as much as the Internet can play a role in sabotaging your mood it can open doors to an endless number of life coaches and spiritual thinkers.

Your Inner Warrior may be fragile now; its voice just a whisper, but with continued positive thoughts and prayers your inner voice will grow stronger and the individual you are meant to be will emerge. A BALANCED TEETER-TOTTER! Carl Jung stated it well: *"Your vision will become clear only when you can look into your own heart. Who looks outside dreams; who looks inside, awakens."*

Every day we encounter situations that we face as a warrior! I challenge you to investigate someone you admire – and learn how they enlightened and strengthened their Inner Warrior. Remember - if you don't love yourself, you will find it difficult to extend a whole heart to anyone or anything else. By creating positive affirmations you ready yourself to face daily challenges. It isn't always knowledge you gain that helps you grow but wisdom from your own experiences. For some, we think adventure is all about discovering something or somewhere new, it really does come down to discovering ourselves.

*"Sometimes you have to reach beyond your grasp to grow inward!"* - Anna Brehm Anderson

Create the Inner Warrior you are meant to be!

# STRATEGIES TO UNLOCK YOUR INNER WARRIOR

1. Where did you find your quiet area? What was it like for you to spend time there?

_____
_____
_____
_____
_____

2. What did you learn about yourself in taking action?

_____
_____
_____
_____
_____

3. Who in your life is an example of a warrior? What qualities do they have that you admire?

_____
_____
_____
_____
_____

# ABOUT ANNA BREHM ANDERSON

Anna is an author, speaker, dreamer, health care advocate, sales professional and warrior who can find enjoyment in textile weaving or getting lost in a great mystery novel. She holds a degree in Hotel & Restaurant Management, is a Certified Meeting Professional (CMP), a graduate of the Dale Carnegie Leadership Training and Disney's College of Knowledge.

As a Stage III Breast Cancer Survivor, Anna remembers her diagnosis and treatments as a time of feeling lost, intense anxiety and being terrified of all the uncertainty. Cancer changed her! By nurturing her spirituality, she grew stronger, was able her to express her emotions and gained inner strength to face life's challenges. The cancer diagnosis has placed her on a journey that she could never have imagined. She is reminded daily, to reflect on her accomplishments, recognize the strides she has taken and celebrate the successes of life, no matter how small.

Her company, Silent Triumphs came to fruition because of Anna's cancer diagnosis. Founding Silent Triumphs' offered her the chance to empower and encourage others to strengthen and build their own hope while facing life's challenges. Her first design, *"Illuminate,"* reminds the wearer, *"Sometimes you have to reach outside your grasp to grow inward."*

Anna resides in the Midwest with her husband and family.

## CONTACT ANNA

- Website: www.SilentTriumphs.com
- Facebook: www.Facebook.com/SilentTriumphs
- Email: Info@SilentTriumphs.com
- Phone: 920-213-1001
- Please go to www.PayPal.com/cgi-bin/webscr?cmd=_s-xclick&hosted_button_id=MV2GRSRA3JEQ8 to purchase this book

## CHAPTER 4
# THE HEART OF OUR FATHER
By Kate Bancroft

There have been many times in my life when I have felt abandoned and alone.

Wondering if God sees what I am going through and, if I am honest, wondering if he cares. Seeking for a connection, a glimpse of his heart, grasping at anything that might lead me to it. Following the wrong advice, walking the wrong path, feeling lost and alone, knowing that I will never be found.

When our children were young we had them in Royal Rangers and Pioneer Girls. What fabulous, fun, scripture focused programs. One challenge we had at church was that the girls far outnumbered the boys. The decision was made to move the boys to a local school gym. Everyone wins. The boys have plenty of room to run and no one is worried about the girls making too much noise.

It was a perfect setup. Almost. We arrived one night to pick up our son. Only to be told by the leaders another parent took him back to church. No answer as to who, only a guess. We drove the 2 miles back to church and began to look for our son. We asked all the other parents who were back with their boys. No one knew where he was or who had brought him back to church. This mama was going into full blown panic mode. How can no one know where my eight year old son is? By this time the adult leaders of the group were arriving back at church. No, all the children had been picked up. They were sure he had to be here. No one knew where. In my mama panic mode, it seemed as no one cared.

At this point, my husband told me to stay at church and keep looking. He was going back to the school. The reality that our son was missing made it almost impossible to breathe. I was looking in every car, asking every person. Fearful I would never see him again.

It seemed like hours before my husband came back with our son. He had found him walking alongside the highway, trying to find his way to church. He had gone to use the bathroom and got turned around in the school. By the time he found his way back to the gym, it was dark, and he was alone.

I am sure my husband physically picked me up and put me in the car. I was going to kill someone. How dare they treat my child like that. How could they have not noticed my child?

Whenever I share this, I can see the *"Mama Grizzly"* arise in the women who are there. Swords drawn, ready to defend their children. Our children are our hearts. You don't mess with our children.

> *Amazing Grace, How sweet the sound*
> *That saved a wretch like me*
> *I once was lost, but now am found*
> *Was blind but now I see*

As much as I love my children, it cannot compare to the depth of love God has for any of us. The Creator of the universe willingly put himself on the cross so I would be found. You would be found.

He seeks after us, not wanting one to be lost.

> **"What man of you, having a hundred sheep, if he loses one of them, does not leave the ninety-nine in the wilderness, and go after the one which is lost until he finds it?"**
> Luke 15:4

Our son was lost and was found by his earthly father. He collapsed into his daddy's arms. His trial of being lost was over, he was now safe.

The groundwork began that night to make sure this would never happen again. No, I was not allowed in that conversation. There is not enough *"holy duct tape"* to have kept this mouth from removing a head or two. It began with the heart of a father. A heart, broken over the trial of his son yet rejoicing at his return. A heart of a warrior birthed in the determination to defend.

The heart of our Father wants each of us to fall into his arms for our trial of being lost is over. He is rejoicing at our return and He has placed in each of us the heart of a warrior.

Yes, you have one too!

You might have to dig it up, dust it off, pry it loose, plug it in or turn on a light but it's there. I think the enemy, you know the one in John 10:10 where is says, ***"The thief does not come except to steal, to kill, and to destroy."*** has done a good job hiding it from us. If those are his three tactics, then we know how to track him.

It is far easier to steal from us than to kill or destroy us. He did it to Eve. She had everything she needed. His conversation led her to doubt. Which, in turn, allowed him to steal her contentment in God's provision for her. Eve, then shared with Adam this new found treat. So began the destruction of their way of life and death entered into the world. It all began with a question.

Is he doing this to you? Has doubt entered in your thinking? Do you not recognize who you are anymore? Are you reaching for food, shopping, alcohol, or media to feel better? Do you feel worn out, beat down, stressed out, and completely depleted? Wondering where God is in all of this?

Here is your wakeup call! It's time to declare *"ENOUGH!"* and defend yourself. To quit living defeated, watching, wondering when it will get better. It's time to unleash our Inner Warrior.

Are you in?

It's time to suit up!

## Wake

Just as he did to Eve, the enemy tells us that God isn't enough for us. That God is holding out on us. Trapped in a cycle of *"looking out for #1," "I am the master of my destiny"* and the *"then I'll be happy."* That we are all have our own truth and it's okay because all ways lead to god. It is time to wake up to the path the enemy has us on and where it will lead us.

> *"Enter by the narrow gate; for wide is the gate and broad is the way that leads to destruction, and there are many who go in by it. Because narrow is the gate and difficult is the way which leads to life, and there are few who find it."*
> Matthew 7:13-14

The narrow path is faith in Jesus.

> *"Now, therefore, you are no longer strangers and foreigners, but fellow citizens with the saints and members of the household of God, having been built on the foundation of the apostles and prophets, Jesus Christ Himself being the chief cornerstone, in whom the whole building, being fitted together, grows into a holy temple in the Lord, in whom you also are being built together for a dwelling place of God in the Spirit."*
> Eph. 2:19-22

Jesus is our Cornerstone. In masonry building, the cornerstone was the first block of stone laid. It determined the size, layout, and direction of the entire building. The cornerstone supports the weight of the building. Remove the cornerstone and the building falls.

Jesus, as our Cornerstone, is the foundation we stand, who we build our life on.

How did Jesus defend himself from the attacks of the enemy?

*"But Jesus answered him, saying, 'It is written, Man shall not live by bread alone, but by every word of God.'"*
Luke 4:4

*"And Jesus answered and said to him, 'Get behind Me, Satan! For it is written, You shall worship the LORD your God, and Him only you shall serve.'"*
Luke 4:8

*"And Jesus answered and said to him, 'It has been said, You shall not tempt the LORD your God.'"*
Luke 4:12

Jesus, the Son of God, used the Word of God to defend himself. Makes sense we should do the same. We need to remember Whose we are and who we are as we prepare to defend.

In 1 Samuel 17, David faces Goliath. Most are very familiar with the account of their meeting. Goliath was so big and David was not. David wins and we all cheer. Somewhere in this David seems to become larger than life. We forget that he faced, fought, and beat several *"you are not enough"* giants before entering the battlefield to face the 9 ft Goliath.

**Not enough giant #1** - His father didn't think of him when Samuel came to anoint one of Jesse's sons to be king. He was unnoticed.

**Not enough giant #2** - His brother, at the battlefield, questioned his motives for being there and dismissed him. He was unwanted.

**Not enough giant #3** - Saul gave David his armor to wear in the battle. What an honor that was bestowed upon David. It didn't fit.

He didn't measure up. He was unworthy.

All of these could have been enough to keep David as a shepherd instead of the king he was called to be. David had a choice to make. He was faced with giants, he could turn tail and run, or he could stand firm on who he knew God to be and fight.

When we are facing the giants in our life, we need to ask ourselves 3 questions.

1. **What does God say about this?** Hebrews 13:8, *"Jesus Christ is the same yesterday, today, and forever"*

2. **What is the giant saying?** You can't do this, you are alone, weak and will never make it.

3. **What am I going to say about it?**

*"And He said to me, 'My grace is sufficient for you, for My strength is made perfect in weakness.' Therefore, most gladly I will rather boast in my infirmities, that the power of Christ may rest upon me"*
- 2 Corinthians 12:9

The thing I know about giants, is that they are loud, big, probably smelly, and seem invincible to us. How we see them gives them their power. When we stand on our cornerstone, we get a *"How Jesus sees them"* perspective and they get a *"Jesus is within me"* boot out of our lives.

## Pray

*"pray without ceasing."*
1 Thessalonians 5:17

For so long I didn't understand how one could pray without ceasing. I am expected to talk to people right? Is this the way God hears me? I must keep praying so it will get to him? So, I would repeat the same thing over and over like a broken record. Dear God, help this person. Dear God, heal that person. That's how I prayed. Until the day I heard someone say you pray, not until God hears you but until you hear from God. Lightbulb!

Psalm 18:4 tells us that our cry comes to His ears. I don't have to wear God out. If you are a mom, you know what I mean. How many times can you hear mom, mom, mom, mom before your eyes roll back in your head and you hide in a closet?

Prayer isn't a *"fast food"* meal with your Father in heaven. It's an intimate time of praise, repentance, asking, and yielding with the Creator of your soul. The word tells us that we will find Him when we seek Him with all our heart. It is in this time with the Lord we hear from Him. Jesus withdrew regularly to pray. His disciples asked Jesus to teach them how to pray. In Luke 11: 2-4, it is a beautiful account of, who God is, praise, purpose, petition, pardon, protection, and finished with more praise. For me, I always thought the teaching of how to pray stopped there. In verses 5-13, we are given a picture of persistence and how much the Father wants to bless us. I have wondered if I have missed many good and perfect gifts because I didn't not sit at His feet and wait. My impatience does not mix well with prayer.

> *"For where your treasure is, there your heart will be also"*
> Matthew 6:21

> *"But seek first the kingdom of God and His righteousness, and all these things shall be added to you."*
> Matthew 6:33

I meet many who are unsure what to pray or how to pray. Prayer is a two-sided conversation with God. You don't need flowery or KJV language for your prayers to be heard. You need an open heart and remember to listen more than you talk. Make time in your day to pray. No soldier goes onto the battlefield without communication from headquarters. It would be foolish, dangerous, and ineffective. That is exactly how I used to start my day. When it was suggested that I get up earlier, I thought they were crazy! Over the past year I have been setting my alarm earlier, bit by bit. I am now up an hour before anyone and the time alone with God in the quiet of my house is priceless! Get up earlier, take part of your lunch time, whatever it takes, it is that important. Pray scripture. If you are battling something, you can go to Bible Gateway or Google and ask for scriptures about sickness, anger, depression, marriage, raising kids……. This is a great way to start. Seek scriptures for what you are battling and memorize them. Put them on three by five cards and carry them with you. Hang them on the fridge, on the mirror, on the tv. Jesus used scripture because He knew it. If it's not in you, it won't come out of you.

Prayer brings clarity to our situations, our struggles, and our lives. Prayer reveals the heart of the Father. It connects His heart with yours and fills your warrior heart to overflowing when you wait upon the Lord.

### Fast

I know, I just lost you on this one! It wasn't that long ago that my eyes would roll back in my head and my ears would shut when someone began to talk about fasting. I didn't understand it, didn't want to do it, so I clung to a statement I had heard somewhere that it was just an old testament thing. I thought who really follows what the Old Testaments say…. Yeah, just Jesus and some of greatest warriors for God ever! I needed that wake-up call!

What causes us to ignore this spiritual discipline of fasting? That we don't know how? That it isn't convenient? We know it's about food, right, but what is it really about?

In January, I began my first fasting experience. I knew I needed guidelines and support, so I joined a Daniel Fast group. For twenty-one days, I ate no animal products, gave up my tea (the tea, for me, was the hardest part) and focused on the study. Why did Daniel fast? Chapter 1: 8-17 tells us the account of Daniel's decision. He was seeking to keep himself separated for God. I did it and loved it. During the fast, I realized how I had been wandering in the wilderness for forty years. I have often chastised the Hebrews for their forty year journey. Thinking of their choices and how could they miss what was right in front of them. Here I am, for forty years, in the wilderness, just steps away from the Promised Land, only to turn back to that which keeps me there. Food.

Here the enemy is stealing my contentment with who I am in Jesus by using food to cover the pain of rejection, loss, relationships, it's the biggest *"not enough"* giant in my life. I had given the enemy the key. He didn't even have to try to break in, I threw the door wide open. I had allowed the rejection and bullying I experienced as a child to be used against me by the enemy to keep me in the wilderness. Overeaters Anonymous uses the acronym BINGE. Most of us binge on something. Food, shopping, alcohol, Netflix. We binge for this reason, *"Because I'm Not Good Enough."*

Let's lock the door and throw away the key on this. Sometimes we are so desperately hungry that the only way to feed ourselves is to fast. Fasting removes food from us for a predetermined time so we focus on God instead. It draws us closer to our Father and gives us a deeper hunger for Him. It brings our flesh under subjection.

How do you fast?

I have used these 6 steps many times to help people fast.

**Pray** - Align your heart with God.

**Plan** - Set your intention for the fast. How long, what food, etc.

**Prepare** - The enemy will come against you. He will.

**Participate** - As Nike says, *"Just do it!"*

**Praise** - Every step of the way. Celebrate and thank God for every victory!

**Process** - Journal, Journal, and Journal a little more.

The clarity and confidence you gain fasting is priceless compared to food that is removed.

## Slay

> *"Then David said to the Philistine, 'You come to me with a sword, with a spear, and with a javelin. But I come to you in the name of the Lord of hosts, the God of the armies of Israel, whom you have defied. This day the Lord will deliver you into my hand, and I will strike you and take your head from you. And this day I will give the carcasses of the camp of the Philistines to the birds of the air and the wild beasts of the earth, that all the earth may know that there is a God in Israel.'"*
> *- 1 Samuel 17:45-46*

We allow our lives to be stolen from us because of three things;

- We forget Whose we are.
- We forget who we are truly fighting.
- We do not engage in the battle.

It's time to stop running. It's time to awaken your Inner Warrior.

We know that we battle not against flesh and blood. We know that Jesus told his followers to Go. We know the weapons of warfare are mighty to bring down strongholds. That we are not given a spirit of fear but of power, of love, and a sound mind. We know the Holy Spirit leads us into all truth. We know God Himself has given us a suit of armor to do battle in.

Are you ready to declare war against the one who is seeking to destroy you and your family?

The greatest battles are fought and won on our knees. Pray.

Seek the Lord with all your heart and separate yourself. Fast.

Draw the Sword of the Spirt, which is the word of God. Which we must read, study and memorize.

Stand fast on the Cornerstone that is Jesus Christ.

Mighty Warrior, let's go slay some giants!

### STRATEGIES TO UNLOCK YOUR INNER WARRIOR

1. Where does the enemy come to steal from you? Where do you feel *"not enough?"* Look up scriptures that talk about this area. Write them out. Read them! Memorize them!

_____
_____
_____
_____
_____

2. Pray Deuteronomy 6:5, *"That you shall love the Lord your God with all of your heart and with all of your soul and with all of your strength."* Ask the Holy Spirit to help you.

_____

_____

_____

_____

_____

3. What action can you take today to grow closer to God?

_____

_____

_____

_____

_____

4. In Colossians 3:12 it says we are God's chosen people who are dearly loved. Spend time today writing that with your name in it. Let that soak deep into your spirit. God chose you and He dearly loves you.

_____

_____

_____

_____

_____

5. Decide to fast! Pick a day and begin. Journal the journey.

_____
_____
_____
_____
_____

# ABOUT KATE BANCROFT

Kate Bancroft understands how to turn your weaknesses into strengths. Kate develops growth, brings hope, and trains women who are fighting the giants of self-limiting beliefs and the food they use to mask the pain. She is committed to walking with these women on their journey to breakthrough. She celebrates that when a giant falls, the true treasure they are is revealed. Kate draws from her 30 plus years in ministry, customer service, business building, and life experiences to impact and transform lives through her coaching, speaking, and writing. Her retreats and workshops provide a space to discover the weapons needed to fight and win against the giants in your life.

Kate is certified through The John Maxwell Team as an Executive Leadership Coach, Personal Growth and Development Coach, and Communications.

Kate is a recovering chocoholic and an eating disorder diva who lives down a little dirt road with the love of her life, her husband Brian.

## CONTACT KATE

- Website: www.SlayingGiantsWithKate.com
- Facebook: www.Facebook.com/Kate,Bancroft.94
- LinkedIn: www.LinkedIn.com/Kate-Bancroft-967559104
- Email: Kate@SlayingGiantsWithKate.com

# CHAPTER 5
# SIMPLY PUT...MY STORY, A SONG, MY PRAISE!

By Chestina Parker Dowgiewicz

**It is said, a person with compassion who understands pain and the consequences of one's action is a warrior.**

**It is said**, that a person who goes into battle without surrendering, overcoming adversity through will, sacrifice, and self-awareness, is a warrior.

**It is said**, those who face impossible situations and survive through keen focus and divine inspiration, is a warrior.

**It is said**, someone who embraces the journey of self-discovery in order to benefit others as well as enlighten themselves, is a warrior.

**It is said**, being a warrior has nothing to do with a physical battle, making war, fighting, or being mean and tough. The battle the warrior faces is a spiritual journey, mastery of one's self, a life commitment, embracing discipline, study, long intense training, and times of sacrifice in comfort and convenience. All with a continuous sense of discovery and understanding one's personal principles and not compromising them.

I never thought my pain, my suffering, my journey, my story would classify me as a warrior; however, it is said, it does. Simply put… my story.

*"Your word is a lamp to guide my feet and a light for my path."*
Psalm 119:105

## **My Story:**

I sat in the tub filled half with water from the faucet and half from the tears that was running down my face. This is not what I imagine my life would be. I lifted my hands up high asking God to take the heaviness away. To everyone on the outside, I lived the perfect life. Nice home, career, husband, child, fancy car, clothes, trips, but inside I was suffocating. *"God please help me, please hear my cry."*

> *"In my distress I called to the Lord;*
> *I cried to my God for help.*
> *From his temple he heard my voice;*
> *my cry came before him, into his ears."*
> Psalm 18:6

Several months later I was woken by a loud explosion sound. I immediately got out of bed looked around thinking someone was breaking into our house. However, everyone else was sound asleep and I was the only one startled by the sound. The explosion was real, my body was shaking, I prayed a simple pray, *"God please protect me and watch over me."* I laid my head back down and went back to sleep.

> *"When I am afraid, I will put my trust in You."*
> Psalm 56:3

A few weeks later we were on our way to Disney. As I jumped into the shower getting ready for our trip, my soap slipped across my chest and out of nowhere I felt this large lump in my left breast, right near my heart. *"Uh,"* I said to myself, *"I don't remember that being there the day before, where did that come from?"* I wasn't feeling quite myself for the past several weeks. I had been fighting a cold for months and didn't think anything of it, until now. I tried to convince myself that nothing was wrong, but, my mind started wandering. I couldn't shake this eerie feeling that was lingering over me. I was trying to wrap my head around it, but I couldn't. I kept thinking to myself, was it residual fatigue from a long pregnancy of being bed ridden for over 8 months. Was it from complete exhaustion, trying to work full time, be super mom, super wife, super corporate, super everything. Was it the internal battle finally raising its ugly head outwardly as I continued to fight off the feeling of loneliness, depressions; okay stop! It's time to go on this wonderful trip where the magic happens and bring me back to my childhood days where I needed to feel free and playful again like a child.

*"Take captive every thought to make it obedient to Christ."*
2 Corinthians 10:5

Finally, I am at my magical childhood place… What! A storm followed me to Disney. Three days into our trip we were facing tornado warnings which was quite unusual in January. Until now I was able to avoid any thoughts on the *"lump,"* but now I was facing it again as we required to remain still in our hotel room until the storm passed. Looking through the sliding glass doors the blue skies and buffy white clouds I awoke to that morning were quickly turning to threating dark gray, black even. The rain was coming down hard and off in the distance you could see mini tornado swirls. The storm outside was a replica of what was happening inside of me as I faced battling my thoughts again in this motionless state. Overwhelmed, I stepped out onto the balcony into the storm, and everything seemed to stop; a complete stand still, silence in the air, and then I saw it, this amazing rainbow. I knew in my spirit it was for me. God heard my cry, but I didn't know what it would entail… ring, ring, ring, the silence was broken, it was my sister calling out of the blue, *"Sis, I felt in my spirit that you need to call the doctors."* and so I did from most the magical place where dreams come true. I made the call.

> *"I have set my rainbow in the clouds, and it will be the sign of the covenant between me and the earth."*
> Genesis 9:13

The *"call"* came on February 14th to be exact, and there was another storm brewing outside. It was a snow storm this time. We were anchored inside our home for the day trying to enjoy the majestic beauty that was happening outside our windows, but this wasn't easy to do, because it was in the midst of us anxiously waiting for the call. The snowflakes were very large where you could see their individual unique patterns. Each one fell majestically from the sky landing gently to their final resting place, one on top of the other. As time went by you could see how their accumulation formed an outline on the branches of the trees and created this radiant glow from their pure whiteness. The scene was so surreal. I was still going through my own internal storm and battling an uncontrollable anxiousness of waiting for my results to come in and yet the actual snow storm itself was demonstrating a calm, peaceful, and orderly moment – a majestic art piece if you will.

> *"Be still and know that I am God."*
> Psalm 47

Many thoughts were running through my head. I needed to remain calm and be still just like the snow outside. Still anxious and needing to grasp on to something of joy, I went to peak into my daughter's room, she was two and a half at the time, she was sound asleep for her afternoon nap. I stood there watching her, how precious and tiny she was, tears started running down my face, *"what if"* I said to myself…, no I can't go there right now. I sat in the rocking chair in her room and began rocking and glancing outside her window to see the snow continually demonstrating what I long to have in my spirit right there and then.

> *"And who of you by being worried can add a single hour to his life?"*
> Mathew 6:27

> *"Cry out to the Lord, He will bring you out of your distress –*
> *He calms the storms, and the waves become still."*
> Psalm 107:28-30

Ring, ring, ring…the silence and tranquility came to an end. I immediately ran to the phone, hesitant to pick it up as the wave of fear and uncertainty made my heart pound to the point of nausea, I answered the phone. It was the doctor; *"your results came in and"* …

I was just told I had stage 3 breast cancer.

Every muscle in my body suddenly gave way. The shock of the news had me falling rapidly to my knees crying from the top of my lungs. *"Why Lord, why…! I don't want to die. I don't want to die. I don't want to die."*

My husband rushed to catch me as he saw the terror in my eyes and heard the whaling sound of my cry. I couldn't breathe, anxiety and fear quickly rushed in attacking every being of my body, mind, and spirit. Our world was collapsing and caving in all around us. My husband still holding on so tight as the words *"through sickness and health"* was about to be tested starting at that exact moment. I continue to lay in his arms in this trance like state chanting I don't want to die God, hear my cry. I don't want to die. We sat there for quite some time soaked and sitting in our pool of tears.

> *"Don't be afraid, because I'm with you; don't be anxious, because I am your God. I keep on strengthening you; I'm truly helping you. I'm surely upholding you with my victorious right hand."*
> Isaiah 41:10

> *"I have engraved you on the palms of my hands..."*
> Isaiah 49:16

The journey began. It was time to fight. It consisted of four months of chemotherapy, intense surgery, and daily radiation for two months straight; this was the battle plan for the sorority sisters with my *"stage."* My physical body was constantly under siege, hair loss, memory loss, body weaken, and the lingering concern of catching a simple cold that could put a kink into the *"battle plan."* The constant stripping of self outwardly and inwardly was daunting. I was tested at every juncture with friendships being broken due to fear, the death of a friend from the disease itself and one of the most excruciating painful breaking point, was never knowing if I was going to see my daughter again, as I had to leave her in the care of my sister as I went to the battle field.

> *"Even though I walk through the dark valley of death,*
> *because you are with me, I fear no harm.*
> *Your rod and your staff give me courage."*
> Psalm 23:4

> *"Trust in the Lord with all your heart, and do not lean on your*
> *own understanding. In all your ways acknowledge him, and*
> *he will make straight your paths. Be not wise in your own eyes;*
> *fear the Lord and turn away from evil. It will be healing*
> *to your flesh and refreshment to your bones."*
> Proverbs 3:5-8

As days turned into months, and months turned into years; It's over eleven years now and counting. I've come to appreciate the rebirthing that was and still is occurring in me. As you can see, I remember the day, the journey so vividly. Every emotion, every feeling; mentally and physically. I am overwhelmed still just by writing this. It's the day, the day I was instantly enlisted in a sorority I never signed up for. An army I never wanted to fight in, February

14th to be exact – Valentine's Day.

> *"I will give you a new heart and a new mind. I will take away your stubborn heart of stone and give you an obedient heart."*
> Ezekiel 36:26

> *"'For I know the plans I have for you,' declares the LORD, 'plans to prosper you and not to harm you, plans to give you hope and a future.'"*
> Jeremiah 29:1

My journey to recovery would awaken a spiritual seed that was planted in me but laid dormant and inactive for quite some time. Little did I know the battle was not only for my life, but for life, and how the mini bursts of battles along the way would have me planting seeds for those behind me, near me and even those ahead of me.

> *"How blessed is he who considers the helpless; The LORD will deliver him in a day of trouble. The LORD will protect him and keep him alive, and he shall be called blessed upon the earth; And do not give him over to the desire of his enemies. The LORD will sustain him upon his sickbed; In his illness, you restore him to health into others."*
> Psalm 41: 1-3

You see, I thought after the argyrias battle with *"C"* (cancer), the war would be over. I didn't know it would be the training ground for the residual battles to come. I call it PTCS, post traumatic C syndrome. I am sure there is now an actual name for it since those in my *"sorority"* are living longer and living healthier lives; *"living beyond breast cancer"* to be exact. But no matter how far out from the day of the battle, the effects of the war still linger. Depression, anxiety, chronic insomnia, physical scarring, a simple cold is no longer a simple cold any more, a pain is not simply a pain any more…it's a constant battle of the mind, and you never know what will trigger it.

> *"Waging war against the law of my mind*
> *and making me a prisoner."*
> Romans 7:23

The residual scars are individualized but the sorority is not. No matter where you are in the journey; this is our sacred bond, we just instinctively know what the other is going through in the inside; it's the silent war that keeps us in a constant warrior state.

> *"But encourage one another day after day,*
> *as long as it is still called today."*
> Hebrews 3:13

My journey catapulted me into something I didn't know was being birth out of me. It was God's divine and unconventional *"road construction"* of which started the day I raised my hands crying out to him and surrendering. It allowed me and continues to allow me to experience Him so differently in the midst of my *"reconstruction"* which is ongoing. I learned what a true warrior is, one who is constantly surrendering daily to dying of self. It took my journey, a sorority, an unsolicited enlistment to make me realize it. In the midst of this impending chaos, I chose to live in faith, and rejoice in God - simply put, because of my story…I AM A Warrior!

> *"The LORD is with you, mighty warrior."*
> Judges 6:12

## A Song:

## Warrior by Hannah Kerr

*Staring down the face of fear*
*Gotta keep breathing*
*When the negative is all you hear*
*Gotta keep believing*
*'Cause in the dark there is a light*
*Your truth it keeps on burning bright*
*Brave enough to fight the fight*
*And shout the battle cry*
*You'll never stop me I'm a warrior*
*When I fall down I get stronger*
*Faith is my shield, His love is the armor*
*I'm a warrior (I'm a warrior)*
*I'm a warrior (I'm a warrior)*
*I'm a warrior (I'm a warrior)*

*Every scar on my skin*
*Is a beautiful reminder*
*Of a moment when I didn't give in*
*And I walked through fire*
*'Cause in the dark there is a light*
*Your truth it keeps on burning bright*
*Makes me brave to fight the fight*
*And shout the battle cry*
*You'll never stop me I'm a warrior*
*When I fall down I get stronger*
*Faith is my shield, His love is the armor*
*I will keep the hope alive*
*I will find the strength inside*

*You'll never stop me, I'm a warrior*
*When I fall down I get stronger*

*Faith is my shield, His love is the armor*
*I'm a warrior (I'm a warrior)*
*I'm a warrior (I'm a warrior)*
*I'm a warrior (I'm a warrior)*
*Jesus make me Your warrior*
*I will keep the hope alive*
*I will find the strength inside*
*I will keep the hope alive*
*I AM A Warrior*[3]

## My Warrior Prayer:

Father, I thank You for the storms of adversity; battles that have cleared a path to the ultimate destiny You have for me, whatever that may be. You have and continue to provide the strength and the endurance to keep my light burning bright, so that others may see You in me. I pray that I may speak of You and share Your word God, more courageously and fearlessly, as I continue trusting in You. When I am tempted to give up or become weary and can't see the end of my current situation; my *"battles,"* God I know You will hold me and I can rest in Your presence. I praise You in the storms; I praise You for the warrior You made in me. Love your daughter Chestina.

## STRATEGIES TO UNLOCK YOUR INNER WARRIOR

1. What is your story that helped discover the warrior in you? (I encourage you).

_____

_____

_____

2. What is your song that celebrates your warrior story? (I encourage you).

_____
_____
_____
_____
_____

3. What inspirational scripture and quotes become your armor and fuel in your warrior state? (I encourage you).

_____
_____
_____
_____
_____

4. Write your personal warrior prayer of praise. (I encourage you).

_____
_____
_____
_____
_____

# ABOUT CHESTINA PARKER DOWGIEWICZ

If you asked Chestina Parker Dowgiewicz to provide a bio 11 years ago she would have started off by introducing herself by her work title and listed all her notable accomplishments in her career and various leadership roles she held.

However fast forward to today; and Chestina will passionately declare who she is; first and foremost a child of God and then proceed to say, a wife, mother, daughter, sister, mentor, inspirational dancer, survivor, entrepreneur, speaker, coach, awareness warrior, Living Beyond Breast Cancer advocate, and Founder of My Ark of Health – literally in that order.

Chestina is on a mission, as she passionately calls it *"market ministry;"* as she shares her personal story from her health battle, her passion to inspire others in her dance, her time commitment to mentoring young entrepreneurs, and even in her advocacy of challenging women and men to make better choices in the daily products through her business she is ministering; even when she is simply *"being still."*

## CONTACT CHESTINA

- Email: 123Chestina@gmail.com

# CHAPTER 6
# THE JOURNEY OF AN INNER WARRIOR

By Jacquie Fazekas

A s the quietness of the universe sinks into slumber, the Inner Warrior is born.

Created by God and conceived between two earthly beings, the birth not yet evident to the world. As the days pass, physical form takes shape. The Warrior learns to rest in patience as she grows moment to moment. For there is nothing to do, but just be. In this state, trust, hope, love, patience, joy, faith, creativity, and non-judgement are seeded in the Warrior. For what else is there? Time seems to stand still in the quietness of just being.

As the weeks go by, the Warrior begins to connect with her senses, some stronger than the others. Hearing sounds awakens the Warrior. She begins to tingle in her body. The beat of her heart keeps rhythm to the sounds. Darkness surrounds her, yet she is able to see light, the light connecting her back to her God. It is an inner light that burns bright. The flow of breath is slow and steady. It is regulated by the current of the water naturally caressing the entire body armor as it grows.

**Those will remain in darkness, until they choose to see the light.**

As her curiosity begins to grow, The Warrior starts to move more. She can feel her body armor taking form and can begin to taste. She savors the new explorations in the womb. Having an appreciation of her existence and knowing her mission, the anticipation builds inside about what lies ahead of her. She begins to imagine a life full of beauty, love, and oneness — for this is all she has experienced. The Warrior quietly rests, breathes, and settles back into peace, just being. Her body armor must gain strength and size before the mission can be launched.

Moments are all the Warrior knows. Moments of joy from hearing a loving voice. Moments of poking and nudging as the outer world slowly tries to connect with the Warrior. Realizing that the voices and sounds are echoing from outside of her, she begins to listen more attentively to them. She anticipates the connection from outside of herself, by rolling and kicking her body armor. Soon, she realizes that her outer body armor has grown and is much stronger than she imagined. Thrusting her feet, she connects with a touch that is insulated, but gives hope of what might be waiting on the outside. Still in darkness, with her eyes closed, she trusts that she is being equipped for the adventure ahead.

Slowly, the Warrior is awakened to the idea of an existence outside of herself. What could that mean for her? The comfort of her current state is a space of love, non-judgement, where just being is valued. Would she be loved? Would she be valued? As she begins to recognize what she is thinking, she starts to question how she is feeling.

Now, she is even more confused. She asks herself, *"Do thoughts come first or feelings?"* She has been feeling her whole existence. The Warrior starts to connect that her thoughts are her feelings — realizing they are one! She had been thinking about peace, love, and contentment all those prior moments, without any outside prompting.

As the outside continues to reach her, she begins to find her thoughts and feelings are slowly revolving around those interactions and less from within. There becomes less time to think from within herself – more from outside her existence. As the moments accelerate, the thought of time begins to form. Her heart races a bit more and the feeling of anxiousness and restlessness begin to appear in her body. *"What is this sensation?"* she asks. *"I feel uncomfortable."*

Days drift by. She seeks her quietness, her oneness, and God's voice for comfort. Just being in silence becomes harder to do. The sounds begin to drown out her access to hearing God's guidance. Her reliance on faith, hope, and trust is all that she seems to be able to grasp on to. The Warrior's body armor has grown in size and is now making it safe for her to pass through to the outer world, the world that has been calling and probing her to come play.

**The beauty of her warrior armor is that she can feel through it!**

The pivotal moment of truth arrives! She thinks to herself, *"Am I strong enough to survive by myself in this new world?"* In typical Warrior fashion, she arrives into the new world kicking and screaming. She must exert her strength to show everyone she is alive and exists! Gasping for water to breathe in and flow, she quickly realizes that there is a new reality to her breadth, air! Her armor is still fueled by water, but now air is a new requirement for life on this earth. New sensations in the body armor appear, like smells and sight. Bright light and unfamiliar smells! She thinks to herself, *"This is not the light I was seeing!"* The Warrior cannot help but think she has lost her connection to her Creator forever.

What once was darkness is now light! Or is it? Smells and taste begin to tempt her in a greater way. Distracted from just being in a state of bliss, she is thrust into doing! She must breathe, feel, cry, eat, sleep, and so much more. She is forced to understand time because her body must do things in a system of timing to survive in this new existence. As the Warrior starts to fight for quiet time, she realizes that her body armor is a powerful machine and it is slowly taking over her thoughts and feelings.

Every day there are new interactions with others. The mother's heart beat and taste seem like the only familiar sensations left from the inner world. The Warrior can feel the love and positive energy from the mother as she nestles up next to her breast and feeds from her inner juices to be nourished. Other beings are not as familiar to her, yet they require her trust, love, patience, and hope-all feelings that the Inner Warrior was born with.

Days quickly turn into months and the outer armor continues to grow. The connection to God becomes more distant with every passing moon. Connections to others become the comforting norm. Stimulation of the senses gets stronger and temptations become more real. The daily feedback and responses the Warrior receives from others begins to shape her behavior. Slowly, just being, is becoming uncomfortable. The outer world is programming her to believe that she has no real power and that her existence is tied to the physical world. She starts to define herself through her relationships with others, their thoughts about her, the stuff she could accumulate, and how she looks. Why should she believe otherwise? She quickly learned she would get exactly what she wanted when she gave in to her temptations. Her thoughts and feelings were being shaped and driven by her sensations, temptations, and pleasure because they felt like love, contentment, and joy. For that is what she craved from birth. They would become familiar and comforting.

Life was quickly shaping all thoughts and beliefs of the Warrior. Failure, rejection, anger, hatred, shame were the new negative feelings taking hold of her thoughts. The Warrior was realizing that negative energies can be powerful in the world. Craving more power, these feelings started to permeate her armor. Positive feelings were being buried deep in the darkness in order to ensure power and survival. The Inner Warrior was becoming weaker and weaker in her power, despite her giving into the negative energies. Before she knew what had happened, she was powerless. In the quietness of her seclusion in the darkness, she looked for the light and sought to hear God, but there was nothing.

# What happened?

She had slowly been trapped by her worldly-self, created in the body armor, also known as Ego. When born into this world, true Self existed in the duality of the Inner Warrior and the outer shell of the ego armor. Just like dark and light exist at the same time, life is made up of many dualities and paradoxes. The Inner Warrior existed before birth without the Ego. Thus, existing in love and harmony. Upon birth, the worldly-self, *"body armor,"* took over to protect the Warrior. Together they are a true Self. What was meant to be protection and to complement the Warrior quickly had become the very thing that attacked the true Self. Thoughts and feelings were now manifested through choice. Choices exist to ensure balance between the worldly-self and the Inner Warrior. Most often the voice of the worldly-self, the ego, is what over powered the voice of the Inner Warrior, causing a severe imbalance of power. It is in this state that the Inner Warrior becomes powerless.

The shift of power started as a little girl. Once she learned to walk, she was in the scrutiny of everyone around her. Walking was not enough, talking needed to follow quickly. When talking was delayed as compared to another child, criticism was quickly levied. She was considered *"slow."*

She seemed to be sicker than the average kid. Always finding herself in the hospital, she began to feel like a broken human. Clearly her armor was defective. She thought to herself, *"What is wrong with me?"* Hearing others talking around her, seemed to confirm that they thought she was broken too.

As the Warrior grew older, nothing got easier. Sickness was inevitable. Not being able to keep up with other kids, solitude became normal. It was counter to her true spirit, but she knew this was part of being broken. Learning to do activities that did not involve anyone, helped with the deep loneliness. Creative hobbies became her comfort and her validation. Her art solicited attention and good words. The association with art would bring her joy.

Creativity was the portal to her soul. For there she found her true self and was able to rest in contentment. As the Warrior had done long ago, she would trust, love, dream, hope, and enjoy patience through the creative process. She could feel pleasure as she lifted the paint brush.

As the Warrior grew older, it became increasingly harder to stay trapped in the basement creating nourishment for the soul. She must face the world that had hurt her so badly as a young child. She thought, *"Must I?"* and then she heard God whisper faintly back at her, *"Yes my dear. You have work to do."*

The Warrior soon learned to adapt and survive, but her compliment of her worldly-self, the Ego, took hold again in order to protect her. However, she quickly discovered that she was once again being suffocated into darkness by her Ego. It had seduced her into feeling good and feeling pleasure. However, with every moment of pleasure came a much longer period of pain in darkness without light.

### Is pleasure worth the price?

When was she going to stand up and reclaim her true self? Was the Inner Warrior dead? In the darkness and silence, she heard the voice from God, saying, *"Trust in me, listen to me, and obey."*

It was a tough thing to even consider. For every time she tried to overtake her Ego, the Ego battled a great inner war, often resulting in a wounded Inner Warrior. As the wounded warrior, the Ego had such power over her that she was weakened by the simplest lifting of a sword. It seemed too heavy to even hold. Certainly, surrendering to her Ego was an easier, less painful path.

Becoming more disgusted with herself and the weakness of her spirit, she would hear in the faint distance, *"Child, stand tall! You were born with and for a purpose. You were created in perfection."* Suddenly, she was positively restless and anxious to hear the voice again. *"Child, I created you to do great work for me. You must fight your Ego. You must overpower it and win the war that rages inside you!"* With a deep breath the Inner Warrior sighed and said, *"Tell me more!"* God did not hold back truths from her. *"You are to find your strength in me! Trust me. Have faith that I am with you with every breadth. I have conquered greater things over many years. With me, everything is possible!"* The Inner Warrior found herself smiling and feeling totally content. Something inside of her could remember her loving spirit that was born from nothing, but with only a detectable thread of existence. During that time, nothing seemed impossible. Everything seemed joyous, loving, and real. For if she could go back to that depth of her true self, could she find that birthed strength? She had given over her very power to Ego, even though Ego never had power at birth. Ego existed at birth, but was never the domineering power. It was simply the outer armor being created. She was going to wage war on her worldly-self, her Ego and reclaim herself!

**She is going to fulfill her mission and purpose.**

She no longer even recognized her true self that was born into this world for a purpose.

Over the years, being so distracted by temptations, she had not been able to hear God's voice. She was not able to learn more about her purpose on earth. Weak, but still alive, the Inner Warrior started to rest more, as she had done in her early years. She would go back to breathing deeply, feeling more, and loving herself without conditions. She knew it would take time and patience, but she would need to cling to love, trust, joy, and hope. The Warrior would need to learn to love, forgive, and be patient with the Ego, if she was to shift the power towards Love. After all, these were her innate feelings that were originally created in her. She knew her Ego would push her to her limits, but she would need to stand in her power, for it is God's power.

### Daily battles waged on with the Ego as the Inner Warrior exerted her love into the world.

Eventually the Ego was silenced and conquered by the Inner Warrior. No longer were the outer temptations a strong hold on the Warrior. The Inner Warrior's power was fueled by knowing there was a greater purpose for her existence and she was going to find out what that was. Her sense of true self was once again defined by Love. Once she felt love, contentment, joy, trust, and hope in herself again, she found it easy to reconnect to her God, for these were the very things that connect her to Him from the start of her very existence. The Inner Warrior battles daily with Ego, for it is a delicate balance required to be able to live with Ego and Love - balance is the power.

### Do you battle with your Ego?

The journey of this Inner Warrior is common. Since the dawn of time, this journey toward living in Love has battled on. Unfortunately, many warriors choose to die in comfort of the Ego and never experience true love. The inner light exists in each warrior but is often snuffed out with overpowering pleasure. It is a journey that has unfolded with multiple endings, all driven from the choice to live and fight Ego or die to Ego.

Like so many paradoxes in this life, we live in darkness until we choose to see the light in the darkness. A warrior must silent the outer voices to hear the inner voices of her true self and of God. The battles that the Inner Warrior wages daily are not easy but fulfilling. They are victories toward completing the mission and purpose on earth, unique to each warrior. For each warrior is only asked to battle in the moment, for there is no other time or place that exists. The next battle is not promised to be victorious, but as more battles are glorious, the war is won.

**Warriors battle on with love.**
**No battle is ever won without Love!**

Each of us has our Inner Warrior waiting to be victorious in this life. Do you feel the calling from within? Do you hold on to hope that one day you will gain the strength to fight the battles? It is only in the quietness of our own thoughts and feelings that we can gain strength and hear the whispers of our Inner Warrior. There we will hear the callings of God as well. Be silent. Be not afraid. Be patient. Be kind. Be hopeful.

**Most importantly, BE Love!**

## STRATEGIES TO UNLOCK YOUR INNER WARRIOR

1. What are the inner battles you are facing?

_____
_____
_____
_____
_____

2. Has your Inner Warrior been trapped into silence by your Ego?

_____
_____
_____

3. Do you spend time in silence each day to connect with your Inner Warrior and to God?

_____
_____
_____
_____
_____

4. Do you love yourself? Practice loving yourself first and then love flows naturally to others.

_____
_____
_____
_____
_____

# ABOUT JACQUIE FAZEKAS

Jacquie Fazekas understands the power of being an overcomer. From surviving life-threatening illnesses and overcoming failure and fears, she has turned her passion into her purpose, which is helping others alleviate stress and disease by making healthier choices surrounding nutrition, mindset, and lifestyle. Her writings, presentations, and coaching encourages and leads others to choose healthier and more fulfilling lives.

Jacquie was born in Canada and moved to Naples, Florida when she was 13 years old. Since then, she has lived in many cities throughout the USA and travelled globally. As a former senior executive for four Fortune 500 Retailers with over thirty years of experience, she brings a diverse perspective and expertise on leadership and life.

With her passion to serve others, she is an Executive Health Coach, Motivational Speaker, and Author of inspirational books. Passionate about health and wellness, she shares her illness experiences with others in hope of sparking more awareness about the importance of living a healthy lifestyle. Today as an Institute of Integrative Nutrition Certified Health Coach and a Certified John C. Maxwell International Coach, Speaker and Trainer, she seeks to continue to serve others in their growth journey, meeting them where they are today and encouraging them along their way — **Everyone can live and lead well.**

## CONTACT JACQUIE

- Website: www.JacquieFazekas.com
- Website: www.YouAreAnOvercomer.com
- Facebook: www.Facebook.com/JacquieFazekas
- LinkedIn: www.LinkedIn.com/in/Jacquie-Fazekas-82824b41
- Instagram: www.Instagram.com/JacquieFazekas
- Instagram: www.Instagram.com/YouAreAnOvercomer1
- Email: Support@JacquieFazekas.com
- Phone: 479-366-2838

# CHAPTER 7
# WARRIOR COURAGE
By Lydia Gates

As I have grown and matured into the young woman I am today, I sometimes look back on how life has treated me.

Most memories I have consist of the good times shared with my closest friends and the family trips we took across the oceans. But, some I keep locked away in the back of my mind seldom being remembered, but nonetheless ever present. These memories are what made me who I am.

At a young age, I learned to understand what cruel meant and what it felt like. When you're young, you don't understand what normal is or what normal should look like. With this in mind, I never knew that I was different. I never knew that *"what I said was any different from what others said"* and that *"the way I looked was any different from the way they looked."*

I tried my hardest as a young girl to fit in. I was very over weight and insecure. I didn't look like a lot of the girls my age and I was picked on a lot for it by my peers. The only thing I wanted to do was be accepted and loved for who I was.

I tried to make friends the best I could and the ones I chose were based on what I thought was the cool crowd. Everyone wanted to be friends with them, but few made the cut. I didn't want to be seen as the girl who had lame friends because I know how looked down upon those *"lame"* friend groups were and I was too prideful to be seen with the lame crowd. Because of this desire to be with the *"it crowd"* of cool people, I set aside what I knew were friendly characteristics and pursued the *"it crowd."*

The first chance I got, I befriended one of the girls who belonged in the *"it crowd."* Before long, I had become well-liked by most of them, or so I thought. I thought it was mostly because of how much I made them laugh. I loved talking to them and being part of their conversations. They always talked about what was going on in everyone's lives, even if they didn't know those people personally. Hanging out with them was great most of the time. I always felt like I had a place to go and people to tell my jokes to.

My closest friends at the time liked to laugh—I didn't know it then, but it was mostly at me. I didn't really understand at the time that I was the designated butt of their jokes. I don't remember what the jokes were or who told them, but I remember the feeling they gave me when they were said. The jokes hurt my self-esteem and made me realize that I was different.

It surprised me that these people, whom I'd come to care about and who meant everything to me, could turn against me so savagely without me even recognizing it. I began to think that maybe I had chosen the wrong friend group, but I didn't put too much thought into it. Not many people can say they are a part of this group, so I never said much to defend myself. I just stayed to myself and would laugh along with their jokes, as if they didn't bother me.

Things began to escalate as the year passed, and I became overwhelmed with the thought of never being accepted. I knew deep down that these people didn't really want to be with me and I was kept there for a *"go-to knee-slapper."* It had gotten to the point where it was impulsive for me to be around them, so I wouldn't be alone. It would seem like that would be the opposite of what I wanted to do, but I didn't have anywhere to go. I constantly followed my *"friend"* group around, in hopes no one would think I was a loner.

The more obsessive I became about not being alone, the more my self-esteem suffered due to my friends harsh ways of communication. But, for some reason, I couldn't leave. I wasn't confident enough to be able to stand alone. I couldn't, for the life of me, separate myself and say, *"The way you treat me is wrong, and I will not surround myself with people who hurt me."*

I was constantly convincing myself that it was okay for them to pick with me and to say those things because they were *"just having fun"* right? I started believing that it was my fault they treated me this way, like I had done something wrong.

I decided to tell them I was sorry, for what I didn't know, but I had to try something. I made the decision that I needed to apologize, so I went to them one day and told them I was sorry if I had ever hurt them. I genuinely tried to make things right. I remember distinctively asking them *"Will you forgive me?"* They said: *"No!"* They would never forgive me, because I was unforgivable. This was my first memory of forgiveness.

Being told I was unforgivable was the worst feeling I had ever had. It was extra baggage I constantly carried around that would only weigh me down. Knowing my mistakes would always be thrown back into my face and never forgotten had hurt more than anything. It was almost a downward spiral from there.

As middle school rolled around, things were even worse. The good news: I had left that friend group and now I was alone. I hated being alone. I wanted someone to notice me and to be friends with me. I took matters to the extreme and began cutting myself. Most people, who do this, say they do it because the pain inside of them has to be released or that cutting is the only thing they can control. Those were two of the reasons I would do this, but I mainly wanted someone to see how much my heart hurt from being alone and being hopeless.

This went on for a year, until my life changed.

After a year of this hopelessness, I knew there was something I needed—something I was missing.

I had been going to church for most of my life. Not every Sunday, but maybe once a month. I never really thought I needed to pay attention to what the man in the front was ranting about. How could he possibly know what I'm going through? It seemed that, after this whole ordeal with these people, I began to listen and try to understand what that man was talking about.

I was at the end of my rope and was running out of hope. Weeks went on and I began to ask my parents what it meant to be saved and why we should be saved. They would explain to me the importance of getting saved and having a personal relationship with God. On the contrary to what my friends had said, I could be forgiven, and by the most important person, Jesus. And my self-inflicted stripes could be healed.

One Sunday, we were visiting my grandma's church. I had made the decision that I had wanted to get saved, but I still didn't know when and where or really how I would do it. They had a visiting preacher from out of state who reached out to me during his sermon. I honestly don't remember what he preached on or what he prayed about. Near the end, he asked everyone if they would bow their heads. He said, *"If anyone here today is unsure of where they'd go if they died today, would you mind raising your hand?"* I paused, and raised my hand without realizing it.

After this, he asked the ones who raised their hands to say a prayer with him while we were standing. As I said this prayer and gave my heart to God, I felt that all those things that those people had said to me were lifted off my shoulders. I don't know how many people raised their hands that day, but I wasn't the only one who was saying that prayer. It was like a chorus of voices was saying it with me. He then asked for everyone who said the prayer to come forward and he looked at me, only me.

After that day, I knew that what they had said about me being unforgivable was untrue. I had been forgiven and my sins would be remembered no more.

A month later I was baptized on September 7, 2014. That week at school, those friends that hurt me from so long ago congratulated me.

Since then, everything hasn't been easy. Not even close. Temptation waits around every corner. The way is straight yes, but it has its ups and downs. Growing up in a world full of *"self-hate and hating thy neighbor"* is difficult.

It took me a long time to find the LOVE that I so desperately needed and to understand what it looked like. The best way I have found to sum it up would be,

*Love is patient*
*Love is kind.*
*It does not envy,*
*it does not boast,*
*it is not proud.*
*It does not dishonor others,*
*it is not self-seeking,*
*it is not easily angered,*
*it keeps no record of wrongs.*
*Love does not delight in evil but rejoices with the truth.*
*It always protects, always trusts, always hopes, always perseveres.*
*Love never fails.*
1 Corinthians 13:4-8

When I found these verses, I made a point to remember them. I know now WHAT I WAS MISSING BEFORE WAS LOVE. I didn't love myself. Now when I doubt God's love, I say these verses and know that He loves me always. I recall this verse anytime I am angry at my friends or myself—anytime I see someone else with something I want or anytime I become self-absorbed. With these verses, I can show someone the true love I wasn't shown those many years ago. I can be a light for someone's dark path that I never had.

In hindsight, I thank those people who hurt me. Without them, I may not have come to Christ because I wouldn't have felt like I needed something. Without them, I would have never discovered my calling to help people my age going through the same pain that I did.

Because of my experiences, I understand that forgiving others and loving them with a true agape love [the highest form of love, the love of God for man, and of man for God] is what we should do for everyone. I know now how important it is to forgive those who have wronged us, because Christ forgives us no matter what we do. I know now how to love people because of how perfectly true love is summed up in 1st Corinthians 13:4-8. I don't hold grudges against them. I pray instead that they will have the same experience as I did when I asked Christ to forgive me.

I sometimes see them and the memories of what they said are seldom remembered, because I chose instead to remember when Christ forgave me and healed my stripes.

## STRATEGIES TO UNLOCK YOUR INNER WARRIOR

1. Do you remember a time when you struggled in school and felt alone? Write down your experience.

_____
_____
_____
_____
_____

2. After reading my story what could you say to yourself to encourage yourself?

_____
_____
_____
_____
_____

3. If you or someone you love is in Middle or High School what insight have you gained from reading this?

_____
_____
_____
_____
_____

4. Who in your life to you need to forgive?

_____
_____
_____
_____
_____

# CHAPTER 8
# WARRIOR RECOVERY
By Lydia Gates

# Trauma- A deeply disturbing or distressing event

After this, many people are never the same and thus greatly affected. Traumatic events can lead to anxiety, inescapable anxiety. It will come in waves and slowly you find yourself becoming restless, distancing yourself from friends and losing all sense of mindfulness. You're just absent. This feeling will permeate through your stomach and engulf you. Your small errors will feel like giant failures and you wonder how many more until you've had one too many. Eventually you will become desperate, begging for anything to take the pain away.

Fortunately, you are not alone. Most of us have all gone through a period of time where we have felt helpless.

As for me, I know this pain very well. After a traumatic event ensued in my own life I was left completely broken. The manifestation of anger and bitterness welled inside almost to the point of consumption. It had felt like I was drowning in a sea of uncertainty. The pain I felt was nothing like I have ever experienced before. I had made up my own mind that it would be impossible for me to heal and if I was, it was nowhere in the near future.

Days went by and that hopeless feeling was still looming over me. Slowly it turned into anxiety that wouldn't allow me to do anything. I was terrified of doing something wrong or failing at something once again. Little did I understand why I was going through such a massive wave of loss. I began reading and studying the Word of God looking for answers. I knew the story of Job very well but in my hour of need God revealed a new meaning of His word to me.

Job, a blameless man before God, familiar with trauma and tragedy had everything taken from him all while his body became crippled and full of agony. His family was taken from him as well as his riches and health. He became so distraught that he wished for his own life to be taken. The accuser came to steal everything he had because the enemy believed that the only reason that Job was faithful was because God had placed a hedge over him. When everything was stripped from him, his wife said he should curse God and die and his friends tried to convince him that he had to confess to sin in his life. Job knew that he was in fact blameless and therefore refused to listen to those people. Because of this he was left alone and suffering. Although his pain ensued, never did he curse God or sin against him. In all ways Job remained faithful to God.

Job had said the terrors overwhelmed him and that as he called out to God, He only looked at Job. Even Job felt like he was being ignored, that his pain was being dismissed and overlooked. The hardest thing anyone must go through is feeling like no one cares. It is hard enough being in pain but it seems to multiply when we are doing it alone. This is a feeling Job knew all too well, he was not only in emotional pain after losing the people he loved but also covered in excruciating festering sores.

Jobs closest friends tried to convince him he had done something wrong. Time and again Job rebuked them knowing he was right. God allowed Job to be tested by those people who seemed wise. Like Eliphaz the Temanite, who spoke to Job saying he was wise and yet knew nothing of Gods plan. We must be weary of these kinds of people because if we listen to their advice or *"wisdom"* we could be setting ourselves up for failure or giving into Satan's plan. When going through a traumatic event there will be people who try and encourage you or give you advice on what you should do. If it is not grounded in the Word of God it should not be trusted nor taken. Your answers will lie in prayer and examples of scripture.

All three of Jobs friends were wrong except for Elihu, who had told Job he was blameless but in all of Gods omnipotence He would also demonstrate His glory and refine Jobs righteousness. Jobs pain was to sharpen his own abilities and to cut out the underlying pride and comfort that Job had with all of his possessions. When God came to Job He told Job to forgive his friends. God had dealt separately with Jobs friends telling them that He wasn't happy with their actions and to go and make sacrifices.

Job prayed with them and forgave them, forgetting all of their transgressions against him. Because Job forgave them, God restored all of his fortunes. Not only what was once lost, but twice as much as what he had had before. Through Jobs faithful suffering he was given more than what he had before. Though his suffering didn't come without doubt and fear he remained faithful.

We look to this story of Job as a hope when we are suffering. We learn that some sufferings are meant to mold and shape us, to weed out the things in our lives that are causing us to stumble. Finding forgiveness will heal those open sores and allow us to move forward in our own season of blessings and restoration.

This new meaning brought healing into my life and allowed me to look at my own pain as an opportunity to be made into a refined version of myself and become more like Christ. The trauma that I had gone through was nothing like the healing that followed, the doors that opened for me to be a blessing to others. I still bare the scars of those events but they allow me to be the testimony to those whose wounds are just now starting to heal.

## STRATEGIES TO UNLOCK YOUR INNER WARRIOR

1. Have you lost someone in your life and your heart is hurting? Read Job 1:13-22.

___

2. Even in the worst of pain, loss, and feeling alone God wants you to know He is with you.

> *"So do not fear, for I am with you; do not be dismayed, for I am your God. I will strengthen you and help you; I will uphold you with my righteous right hand."*
> Isaiah 41:10

3. What are some scars that you carry with you? How could you turn that story from the pain of getting the scars to something positive and as a learning opportunity?

___

4. You have a chance to start over. What do you need to let go of to begin again?

_____
_____
_____
_____
_____

# ABOUT LYDIA GATES

Lydia Gates lives in Lincolnton North Carolina and has a passion for literature and fine arts. In her spare time she plays clarinet and writes poetry.

Recently she was inducted into the Beta Society that represents her ability to be a leader in her school community. In the fall of 2018 Lydia was accepted in UNC-Asheville for the 2019-2020 school year.

Her continued hopes are to lead youth her age through life's challenges.

To have Lydia come and share her story with your organization reach out to her on Facebook at www.Facebook.com/Lydia.Gates.56 or email her at LydiaMGates@gmail.com.

## CONTACT LYDIA

- Facebook: www.Facebook.com/Lydia.Gates.56
- Instagram: www.Instagram.com/Lydiaa.Marie
- Email: LydiaMGates@gmail.com

## CHAPTER 9
# RISE UP:
# KINGS AND QUEENS OF GOD!
By Paula Pierce

# **❝ Arise and set forth on your journey.**

*Take up your armor and your sword! Do not fear men, nor what they can do to you, fear the Lord your God! Know <u>I AM</u> the <u>GREAT I AM!</u> I will lead your steps, the path before you is the path I have predestined for you to walk. You will war, and you will be victorious as you learn the strengths you have in me. Do not fear. The battles you face belong to me, for my Glory, for my purpose. And I will see you through each of them. Keep your head held high, <u>EYES ON ME</u>, for I am your strength. I am your leader. I will sustain you. I will propel you. And I will have the last say in every situation."* Thus, sayeth the LORD.

This is the word I received from the Lord into my spirit as I began to write my chapter within this book! What an exciting word from our Heavenly Father! What a knowledge to behold: the creator of the entire universe, cares enough for **OUR** cares to talk with us!

What a revelation: To know we were **INTENTIONALLY** and **PURPOSEFULLY CREATED** by the hands of God! To know we are more than a clump of cells from our biological parents' DNA, that EACH and EVERY ONE of us have been breathed life into by **GOD HIMSELF! Wow!**

I've told my story recently within the pages of a book God placed into my spirit to write, *"To Mend The Broken."* I have also told it to anyone who would listen. Therefore, I confidently assumed the chapter for this book would be something of the sort in which I've previously talked about. However, the words I'm writing now, are an entirely new revelation!

As God has stretched my spirit, tested my faith, purged my heart, and pushed my endurance, I have come to know who I am on a level I've never known before.

**I now know MY GOD and MY IDENTITY in a way I never imagined.**

I've known God all of my life…literally…I was raised in a home full of the Word and parents who prayed in tongues. I remember vivid tent revivals while growing up; some weeks we would attend a different church service every night!

I gave my heart to Jesus, accepting him as my Lord and Savior, when I was only seven years old. Soon after, a hunger birthed within my heart to have more of God within my life and I sought after the Holy Ghost. God blessed me with His spirit and the gift of speaking in tongues when I was fourteen years old at a small revival in a little church of Berea, Kentucky; it was the greatest feeling I'd ever known. It was as if I had been set on fire from the inside out, full of raging electricity to fulfill the calling upon my life, all while being submerged in the warmest, most-safe-feeling embrace one could ever imagine.

**I still cannot find a comparison to how it feels to enter into God's holy presence!**

Soon after I received the Holy Ghost, people began commenting on the *"glow"* that perpetuated from my being. Time after time, I began to hear people say I was a warrior for God! As I sought him and his ways, God increased my wisdom and knowledge and people became captivated by how mature my conversations would be concerning things of the Lord.

As a teenager, I was on the brink of realizing my **TRUE IDENTITY** in Christ; on the brink of KNOWING WHO I WAS CREATED TO BE! Which is why it shouldn't have come as a shock when the devil warred full-force against my mind to ensnare my thoughts with chains of **confusion, condemnation, and inadequacy. I lost my identity before ever even realizing what it was!**

Fast forward through the next seventeen years, as I remained on a roller-coaster-cycle of confusion while I tried every vice within my reach for the acceptance and validation I greatly sought. (That which my Heavenly Father was constantly trying to give me!) I bounced from failed relationship to failed relationship, job to job, friendship to friendship…trying to validate the worth I sought on the inside!

**I was seeking wholeheartedly for an identity which I tasted a small glimpse of as a teenager and felt so cruelly snatched away by a heartless enemy!**

Even though I saw great miracles during those seventeen years of my life, none of them were enough to tear the veil which blinded my eyes to the truth. This statement can sound harsh to those who know me personally as I witnessed such things, but, it's an honest statement as I hadn't acknowledged my identity in Christ yet.

You see, I've experienced the power of God as I prayed over my dad's lifeless body laying within my arms on the day the enemy attacked his heart! I welded the Sword of the Spirit in a way I never knew I could! Then, I watched life spring forth within his skin as he rose back up!

I've also held the hand of a close friend as she laid unconscious in ICU and doctors began preparing her family for *"the inevitable."* The room was cold. I literally smelt death within the air, and could feel no life whatsoever in her hand as I held it. But, instead of saying goodbye, I felt an empowering on the inside to anoint her and speak life into her as I prayed in the spirit. Within two weeks, she was miraculously released from the hospital!

I've carried my six year old child within my arms as his legs stiffened from an unknown pain which had caused him to not be able to stand nor walk, as doctors pointed towards a diagnosis of childhood leukemia. I had to make a choice immediately, accept or rebuke the symptoms from upon my child. I touched his legs, held him close, and warred in the Spirit against the enemy. Even though he had been sick and in excruciating pain for a week, his symptoms disappeared within twenty-four hours and his blood tests came back negative for cancer!

And I've sat in an office frightened, as the doctor explained she FELT I had an incurable disease which medicine needed to be prescribed immediately (even though no symptoms were present whatsoever, she *"just knew"* I had it). Immediately, I heard the Holy Spirit lead me to rebuke it. Not only rebuke it, but rebuke the doctor as well and was told to not talk of it after the appointment that day. So, I did as I was led, only to have the doctor become irate with me, calling me *"ignorant"* and *"stupid"* as she told me to leave the office! I waited in faith for five days, for the phone call containing my negative test results, which ultimately came directly from the doctor herself as she apologized for being so rude. She said she didn't know what came over her that day because there weren't any symptoms, but for once in her profession, she was glad a patient didn't accept the diagnosis. Amen!

### God is FOREVER FAITHFUL to the prayers of his WARRIORS!

Understandably, people have often commented on the **WARRIOR** within my Spirit and assumed I was already walking in the knowledge of **"IT."** However, even though my flesh has gave way to my Spirit in times of emergencies, I had yet to open my heart fully to God's purpose in my life and walk within it on a daily basis. That is, until the last week of July 2018.

I had just finished my book, *"To Mend The Broken"* and felt led to print a hard-copy of my manuscript so I could deliver it personally to the publisher versus electronically. All week, God had used my ten year old son, Samuel, to confirm his guidance to me, by speaking specific words to Samuel that He'd already shown me. By the 28th of July, I could feel within my Spirit an overwhelming need to follow God's directions exactly as they'd been given. Therefore, despite the fact my husband reacted harshly towards my obedience, I refused to allow anything to stand in the way of completing it!

**God was BIRTHING my IDENTITY that weekend!**

In my heart, I knew a domino effect would come from my choice of obedience, however, I had no idea the ripples that would begin to flow. As a mother of three, I had no clue what to do in the vehicle by myself for an almost six-hour drive that didn't involve singing along with little voices or pointing out construction on the side of the roads…

So, I decided to plug my phone into the radio and stream the latest sermon from my favorite online preacher: John Gray. He'd just begun a new Sunday series called, *The Vision Series*, and I was beyond excited to listen to it.

Within the first thirty minutes of my journey, I was crying out to God as I agreed with the word I was hearing! My heart was so heavy for the husband I left behind and I knew I would have to make changes within my life once I came home. However, I committed to focusing on God alone for the overnight trip. As I called out to God, as I agreed with the prophesy the man of God was declaring, a loud noise began to stir deep within my Spirit and suddenly birth itself out through my mouth.

**I have never made such a sound in all of my life!
I immediately knew it was my Warrior-Cry!**

Tears streamed down my face, as I continued to scream *"YEEEESSSSSSSSS!!!! YES, GOD, YES! HAVE YOUR WAY! HAVE YOUR WAY! YEEEEESSSSSSS!!!!"* I've never felt more liberated, than in **THAT** moment! I've never felt more weightless, than in **THAT** moment! The louder I cried out to God, the stronger I felt God's Spirit growing within me.

Out of all of the moments I've yielded the Sword of the Spirit within my life, none of them felt as **EMPOWERING** as in **THAT** moment. For the next five hours, I traveled the curvy highway to North Carolina, praising God in a way I can only imagine is a tenth of the percent of how I will praise him once I am in Heaven!

I spent the evening in heartfelt conversation with my publisher, Tricia, as we bonded deeply over what God was doing within our lives. The next morning, I awoke with an expectancy in my Spirit as Tricia asked me to accompany her on a small trip. I wasn't sure what to expect, but I was excited. We enjoyed our conversation like two-long-lost friends as we made our journey to the base of a mountain and parked; I could hear the water as I walked from the car towards the trees that lined the road.

### Once we past the clearing, I could see a beautiful waterfall. Moravian Falls.

It wasn't a large waterfall, it didn't cascade down in sheets of powerful, white water and I'd definitely seen more impressive falls before. However, something about it called to me. It stood as a solid, two-tier rock, stretching fifty-foot wide and almost sixty-foot tall. It's water, though not cascading, ran mightily down its surface into a calm pool at the bottom.

As I stood next to the gentle stream flowing from the base of the falls, I heard Tricia's voice next to me. *"You can walk closer,"* she stated. *"Take some time to journal, write whatever God lays on your heart."*

I stood nervous, *what am I supposed to write about?* I thought, immediately followed by thankfulness. *Lord, I've never had a friend encourage me to just sit and listen for your voice! How nice is that?!* Even though I hadn't journaled since a teenager, I bought a new planner/journal recently and brought it with me, just in case it was needed. Unbeknownst to me, that was one of the best decisions I could've ever made!

I walked through the shallow stream and onto the other side, nodding to a family that was eating lunch at a nearby picnic table, and made my way towards the base of the waterfall to an abnormally large rock. I climbed upon it and sat mere inches from the flowing water, as I stretched my legs in front of me and placed my notebook upon my lap.

I prayed and asked God to speak to me, then I praised him: praised him for who he is, for his never-ending supply of mercy and grace, for loving me even during my unlovable moments. Before I knew it, I'd written an entire page of praises to my Heavenly Father.

Then, as the sun beamed warmly, it was as if the atmosphere shifted and I penned these words: *"I will answer the call before me. I will walk blindly into the unknown for my steps have been predestined and my God is forever Faithful! He will NOT leave me, NOR forsake me! He is forever FOR me! I will run and NOT grow weary. I will walk and NOT faint! I will pick up the armor before me, I will take my place on the battle line!"*

I closed my eyes, listening from within as the sound of the steady, unimpressive flow of water began to change into a loud, roaring current. I immediately opened my eyes, to see the same steady stream before me, which didn't match the rushing sound I heard. So, I closed my eyes again and prayed for God to have his way, as

I felt his warm embrace surround me. Within his presence, I could feel the rushing waterfall flowing over top of me as it washed away the heaviness of my past and regenerated strength from within.

**It was a feeling like none other! I felt as if I was submerged within the mighty waterfall of God's Holy Spirit and a new boldness was born:**

### I WILL NOT: <u>BACK DOWN, STEP DOWN, SHUT UP, GIVE UP, OR GIVE IN!</u>

### I WILL: <u>DRESS UP, SHOW UP, LOOK UP, SPEAK UP, AND STEP OUT!</u>

Within this newfound boldness, I wrote another page and completed a live video for my online ministry. God showed me in that exact moment, he won't always stand loudly within my life, saying *"LOOK AT ME."* Rather, he will be tucked away quietly, hidden amongst the trees and mountains, beckoning me to draw closer to him and seek his presence.

If my trip to North Carolina would've ended there, at Moravian Falls, I would've been completely satisfied within my heart and Spirit. However, God seeks to give us abundantly **MORE** than what we could ever think or ask. Therefore, his blessings continued, as Tricia and I made our journey to the top of Prayer Mountain.

The closeness I felt with God at the base of the Falls, was as only an inception for what was to come on Prayer Mountain. As we traveled to the top, I was somewhat reserved in my expectation for our visit. I listened intently, as Tricia spoke of the many miracles people had witnessed on top of the very mountain we were traveling up. However, I felt God could (and would) perform miracles everywhere, so, I didn't understand why people would seek a certain location to experience them.

However, once we parked the vehicle and found seats overlooking the breathtaking view, I thought, why not? I'm here. I might as well just talk to God and allow him to have his way. So, I began to play my worship playlist from my phone softly, as I sought God's presence. Within the first song, as I placed my pen to my notebook, I could hear the still, small voice of God speaking soothingly to my Spirit:

*"Behold, I make all things new. Your former life has passed away, just as your heel print set within the sand. I will wash the past away with the mighty power of my Spirit flowing as the mighty oceans across all of your past hurts and mistakes.*

*Do not fear the unknown, for I AM the known!*

*Do not fear the journey, for I AM the destination!*

*Do not fear the hurt of what men can do for I AM the healer, the protector, the shield, and the strong tower!*

*This life I set before you, is the life in which I created you for. This is your purpose. I will sustain you. I will guide you. I will provide for you. You will want for nothing and your children's children will call you blessed! Accept this Word my child, for it is so!"* Says the Lord.

I was so moved by the words he spoke into my spirit, that I praised him quietly as tears streamed down my face. Is there a connection with this place and your heart, my Lord? I asked him quietly. Forgive me for not believing.

Just then, I heard my name being called from behind and turned to see Tricia sitting in a chair as a couple stood next to her. I quickly walked towards them, noticing it was the same couple I had felt compelled to offer prayer for when we first arrived, but quickly discarded the thought as they looked deep in concentration.

The four of us introduced ourselves as the gentleman held up two pieces of paper with writing on them, one for Tricia and one for myself. God had given him two distinct prophesies concerning Tricia and I, and he intended to share them with us.

I was beyond moved, as he read aloud the Word God had given to him for me: *"You have such a chipper personality, you make others laugh with ease...you will see the life you want manifest...feelings of weariness will fade...loneliness on the inside will diminish...Relaxation, Peace, and Joy will abound...Press forward, you will meet Todd White and Misty Edwards face to face...God has your heart, it's beautiful...you will see much fruit from this past season...God is more real than you realize... Your lips are sweet...you speak with purity...God brought you here to refill you...Expect great Joy!"*

I'd never met this couple in my life, never spoken to them, yet they knew intimate details from my heart. **No doubt in my mind, God had spoken that day!** As we lingered for a moment, the gentleman continued.

*"As I looked at you, I saw a hue of purple radiating from you, so I asked God what it meant. He said it is your royal bloodline, you are of royal descent and you are to remember your position in Christ. Acknowledge your Royal Identity and walk within it."*

*"I also see a teaching anointing upon you,"* he said. *"You must teach, you have the voice for it and the anointing I feel is overwhelming. When you speak truth, you speak it so sweetly people accept it easily. Don't stop doing that, it's a gift."*

To say that God moved in a mighty way during my trip would be an understatement! I believe with every ounce of my being, that I've only touched the surface of the life God has planned for me! That weekend not only opened an opportunity to collaborate within this book, but it also opened the opportunity for my son to write a chapter within this book as well! God strategically placed people where he wanted them and now he is getting ready to do something AMAZING!

Once I came home, I sought God what to do about my marriage as Samuel and I both went to work quickly concerning our chapters. I didn't want the experience I had, to have only been one-time. I wanted the feelings I felt: the EMPOWERMENT, the BOLDNESS, **the HUNGER for GOD'S PRESENCE to last indefinitely!**

Over the next few weeks, my hunger began intertwining with the Holy Spirit, birthing my true identity in God as I sought his face! I consistently read over the prophecy I had been given on Prayer Mountain, as I asked God to help me acknowledge who I am, who I'm created to be! During this time, is when God gave me the revelation I sought after:

## I AM A QUEEN IN THE COURT OF HEAVEN!

See, for the past seventeen years, I have identified myself as a *"daughter of the king,"* a princess if you will. One who was spoiled, immature, and needy; I wanted what I wanted whenever I wanted it, while never counting the costs. I knew who my Father (God) was, therefore I walked in the knowledge of belonging to him, but I lacked boldness of my authority! Whenever a split in the road presented itself (Choose God's choices or chose my own), I would continue with a princess mentality and shrink from the battlefield before me.

However, God has been calling me to mature in my knowledge of my TRUE identity! To associate as a Queen, I would henceforth acknowledge the authority my words carried, the weight my presence exhumed, and the bloodline in which I came from…at **ALL** times! Through Jesus' blood, we have **ALL** become joint-heirs with him! Therefore, we are **ALL KINGS and QUEENS**, we **ALL** have the same authority as Jesus! And when it comes to warfare:

A true **KING** and **QUEEN** will take up their **ARMOR** on the **FRONT LINE!** Their very presence will create a stir of enthusiasm amongst the warriors alongside of them and will invoke fear into the enemy before them!

## KNOW WHO YOU ARE!!!

## YOU ARE ROYALTY!!!

## YOU ARE A WARRIOR!

### STRATEGIES TO UNLOCK YOUR INNER WARRIOR

1. When did you *first* realize your true identity in Christ? What did that moment feel like?

_____
_____
_____
_____
_____

2. Have you ever had to make a sacrifice in order to be obedient to God? How did that turn out? If not, would you be willing to? Why/Why not?

_____
_____
_____
_____

3. When you imagine a WARRIOR, what do you see? Write it down descriptively! Can you see yourself in that image?

_____
_____
_____
_____
_____

4. What's one thing you want more of: BOLDNESS? PROPHESY? SUPERNATURAL ENCOUNTERS? Use this space to write a prayer about it!

_____
_____
_____
_____
_____

5. Now that you know you're of royal descent, what adjustments will you make within your life to show that?

_____
_____
_____
_____
_____

6. Use this space to write a declaration which you will speak every day, encouraging your spirit to rise to the call of being a WARRIOR for GOD!

_____
_____
_____
_____
_____

# ABOUT PAULA PIERCE

Paula is a thirty-two year old native of Kentucky who resides with her family in the small town of Mount Vernon. She has always cherished a love for writing, ever since a small age and has been published multiple times within local establishments. Her most recent accomplishment was the completion of her first book, *To Mend The Broken*, as well as her weekly & uplifting, live videos on her various ministry pages!

Her heart has always drawn out the best from people within life: seeing the glass full & overflowing while noting the silver-lining within every situation. She is exceptionally gifted and talented with her words, as well as her spirit of encouragement towards others! She seeks for God to use her to help mend the broken places within the hearts of humanity while setting people free from the strongholds of their past!

Along with her book, she also speaks upon a variety of platforms including women's meetings, substance abuse/rehabilitation programs, high school assemblies, youth rallies, etc. and will continue to broaden the stages in which she speaks for the Word of God. If you would like for her to speak at your event, please use one of the contact methods below.

## CONTACT PAULA

- Facebook: www.Facebook.com/MendedWarrior
- Twitter: www.Twitter.com/MendedWarrior
- Email: BlessedPierce@icloud.com

# CHAPTER 10
# THE WARRIOR STRENGTH DISCOVERED

By Amanda Powell

**F**or as long as I can remember I have been a people pleaser. I want to be liked and never disappoint.

As I have continued to grow in my business and my leadership I have discovered how much this thinking made me unhappy. I tend to take on other people's emotions and stress, making them my own. I make choices I don't want because I don't want to disappoint others. I stress when I finally make a decision because I want everyone to be happy and not be upset by a decision that I make.

Living this way has been incredibly stressful and growth limiting. Why do I care so much? Why do I let others have so much power over me? How do I make choices that make me happy? I struggled for so long and still have times where I can't make choices because I don't know what I want. I find myself in this position because what I want may be something completely different then what is *"expected of me."* I do not think I am alone and I want to be empowered by my choices. Choices that I can make strongly, confidently, and that make me happy. I want my daughter to be confident in what she thinks about herself and how she feels more then what others think about her. As I sit here today I can see how much I have been changing over the years to become more of the person I want to be. It has been a slow process but so life changing. I know where my strength comes from. My strength comes from God alone. **"God arms me with strength, and he makes my way perfect."** Psalms 18:32 (NLT)

When I start to swerve off and spend more time pleasing others than myself I sit back and think of where God wants me to be. I ask for his guidance to become the person he created me to be. I do want to be liked and make people happy but no longer at the expense of my happiness or health.

In 2016 my husband, who serves in the US Army, left for his 5th deployment while my real estate business was still growing. I was failing forward daily with learning and leadership and I wasn't giving my best to my wonderful kids. My kids were getting what was left of me after a long day of working. I wasn't taking care of myself, I would only go to the doctor every few years, I wasn't exercising and I didn't really eat (does cereal count). In December 2016 I was finally fed up. I was tired and worn out and over it. I wanted to be happy and healthy and have my cup filled so I could fill up my kids instead of my cup being empty and my kids getting nothing.

## A Busy Time

Before we go further, we must go back. Back to a time of when I started to figure out who I was going to be. I was in my first year of college with a busy schedule. Full load of classes, twirling with the band, and holding down three part time jobs. I loved it all. I love being busy and helping others and figuring things out. School really fit me. In November of my freshmen year I met the man who would become my husband. He was truly the man God created for me long before I was born. Three months later he proposed and seven months later we were married. We married in September and I needed to finish the semester in Texas before moving to our new home where he was stationed at Fort Polk, Louisiana. We started to build our life as a married couple finally getting to live together in December and in March everything changed in a heartbeat. I remember very clearly getting a call at the job I just started and my husband told me I needed to come home. Little did I know how fast things would move and change after I got home. My husband was a scout and alerted that afternoon his unit would be deploying in five days to Iraq.

I was twenty years old, newly married, and living in another state. For the next year I spent little time in my hometown and then most of my time in our Louisiana home finishing my associates degree. I was fortunate to have amazing friends who were going through the same deployment. I had the option of throwing myself a pity party or building my strength so that I could support my husband.

I received a 5 minute phone call once a month and several letters from my husband. Even though I would have loved more I was so grateful to even have that. I would think about how my great grandmother didn't hear from my great grandfather for two years during WWII, so I had nothing to complain about. My husband returned home a year later, and a few short months after we decided we were ready for children.

## A New Chapter In Our Lives

We were lucky enough to get pregnant with our daughter quickly. While pregnant with her my husband received orders for recruiting duty. We were beyond blessed and were actually stationed in my hometown. This allowed us to have our daughter in the same hospital I was born. Being with family was so nice and helped a lot as we lost my step mom just a few months before I delivered. I did my best to be strong for my dad, brother, and sisters as it was a devastating time. I helped with the funeral and housing arrangements as staying busy is how I deal with my emotions. The next few years were filled with our daughter growing up, me losing a baby, and then receiving the gift of our son. I stayed home with both kids for the first few years and I am so thankful I was able to do so. Sometimes I look back and wish I would have stayed home longer and other times I see the opportunities that we have had by the timing of when I chose to start working. When my son was four months old he had to have surgery. He spent the first few months of his life barely growing and not holding any food down. He was in the 5th percentile for height and weight. After waiting for months to see the specialist, it took ten minutes after being in the room before being admitted immediately. The next ten days are almost a blur. Test after test, almost sending us home, and then surgery. My son turned out to be such a strong little boy. After three years with my husband on recruiting duty we moved to Fort Knox, Kentucky. We were only there for a short thirteen months. Then came the longest period my husband was gone. He went to a school for five months, came home for a month, and then deployed again for a year. The kids and I chose to move back to my hometown since it was such a long time. This is when our son dealt with his next health issue. At the age of two he hemorrhaged ten days after having his tonsils and adenoids removed. That was probably one of the scariest experiences I have gone through. Both my daughter and son were so strong. My husband was deployed and this all happened the day before our daughter turned five. Having family near also made a big difference. I am also grateful that his health issues, even with multiple surgeries, have been limited and I continue to pray for all children that are going through much more.

After my son's surgery the next few months were filled with kid activities, working on my new real estate business, spending time with family, and preparing for another move. After my husband came home we left for our new home in Fort Leavenworth, Kansas. We were only there thirteen months as well, but it ended up being one of our favorite locations. We joined the on post church and I joined Protestant Women of the Chapel (PWOC), the women's Bible study group. Being part of PWOC was such a time of growth for me. I was fortunate enough to lead a Bible study, serve on the board, mentor, and be mentored by amazing women.

Having other strong women to lean on I think is crucial in this military life. Actually having strong women to lean on no matter what is important. You become a reflection of the five people you spend the most time with. Have you looked at your sphere lately? Are you spending time with people who lift you up, hold you accountable, and are there for you no matter what? Building lasting friendships definitely helped me in times of stress, times of joy, and when I needed more strength to keep going.

## Another Move

Just before Christmas while living in Kansas my husband was informed, he would be receiving orders to Fort Meade, Maryland. We went home for Christmas and New Years with the family, and when we returned back to Kansas, we had about three and a half weeks to plan our move to Maryland. It all moved so fast but I have always enjoyed fast pace timelines. When we arrived in Maryland we found a rental and got our daughter into her new school. I was working on finishing my Bachelor's degree at the time but then also decided to obtain my Maryland Real Estate license. I tested and received my Maryland Real Estate license in May and began working. Maryland real estate was very different from Texas real estate. The coverage area was much larger, the pace was faster and I was learning all through the busy summer months. Not long after getting to Maryland we found out my husband would be going on another deployment. We did what we always do, we stayed strong and stayed busy. In September of that year I graduated with my Bachelor's degree and my husband left for a 6 month deployment.

We were so thankful it was shorter than any other deployment we had gone through. A few months later we moved into our new house just before Thanksgiving and my real estate business was starting to take off. From the end of 2012 to 2017 our time was filled with sports, school, long hours helping real estate clients, and two more deployments. In all of that I found myself putting in time to take care of others. Sometimes people saw what I was doing and sometimes they didn't. The few hours of sleep, doing what I could to make sure others were taken care of or happy, and going weeks on end with no break. I did this type of routine for years. A lot of it came from me wanting to take care of others and some of it came from wanting to be liked. I do not regret the time and energy put into others. Some of it has been a blessing and some of it has helped me learn and grow my leadership and skills. When I look back, there are times that I put clients or colleagues over my family and myself, because I wanted to help. My family is most important to me and it took me some time to stop putting them second to people who may not remember my name in a few years. There are things I missed out on but I no longer let that hold me down with regret. I remind myself that I can control today but not yesterday and I do my best to give my best self to the ones I love. That includes me.

## Finding Me Again

I started by joining a gym. I had so many excuses over the years of why I didn't go to the gym or why I would start and only last a few days or few weeks. I would complain about my knees, bad back, or the fact that I get bored really easy. I have allowed these excuses to hold me down and mess with my mindset. So I decided to go at it again. I joined a local gym that was about five minutes from my house. Excuse one down, no excuse about it being too far. The gym I joined was low in price and had everything from machines, weights, classes, training, and even a theater room. Excuse two of cost down. When I decided to give the gym a shot again I wanted to do it right and find what worked best for me.

I joined in with the group training that the gym offered versus just doing the classes. Again I get bored really easy so when it comes to regular classes I always find myself ready to leave within about twenty minutes. I found myself enjoying the group training for a few reasons. It was a smaller group, every minute or so we were doing something different, I was getting cardio and able to do weights. I started with the goal of going 2-3 days a week.

I decided to order premade foods from a company that specializes in small portions with a variety weight loss and protein for strength building. This was due to the fact I don't cook or eat right (again, cereal counts right?). By going to the gym I found myself decompressing from work and coming home eager to spend time with my kids because I had the ability to let go of some stress. I didn't come home and need a break or just wanting to be alone. Instead I wanted to play with my kids and enjoy my time with them. I have been consistent with the gym since I started and it has made a world of difference. Not just in my weight and health but my energy and attitude. Now that my daughter is older she even enjoys going to the gym with me and my son can't wait to go. When my husband doesn't exercise at work he gets to go with me. Being able to do this together as a family has been really enjoyable.

### Is There A Balance?

Joining the gym was a great step for me. I love my business and helping clients so much, but I was so tired by the end of the day. I built my business with a goal to help military families with their real estate needs and I found myself working to give them as much of me as possible, but it was wearing me down and my family was getting less of me. Finding a balance in the real estate business is so hard but I knew I needed to figure something out. Once I was committed to working towards being the person I wanted to be, and the mom I wanted to be, I was able to become more purposeful in my schedule. I found myself with full free weekends to spend with my kids and days here and there during the week that I could take for myself. I didn't have to stress about running errands or taking something away from someone because I couldn't fit it all in my schedule. I learned I could say no to somethings in order to say yes to others. There are still days when I work on this but I can see by making the choices of not doing everything, so much has changed. I do not think that complete balance is possible but being happy in my schedule and my choices has allowed me to keep my cup fuller.

By making these choices while my husband was deployed it

allowed me to get my mind, spirit, and body in a place of peace and happiness before he returned. We were lucky enough to be able to talk during his deployment which really helped me as he is always so supportive. Since he came home, and me becoming more of who I wanted to be and letting go of things I couldn't control, we were able to grow deeper in our relationship. I have found that I can be strong, productive, take care of others, and still take care of myself. By letting go of what I cannot control and realizing I do not need to control everything, I have been able to live more of the life I want to live. Life is to short and only God can control the path. I am focused more on living daily instead of just getting through the day and on to the next. I don't have to be only a mom, an army wife, business owner, or friend. I can gladly be those simultaneously with pride and not lose myself at the same time. I have been getting better at not comparing myself to others highlight reel online or my speed of growth to others. I don't have it all together but I am ok with that as I am growing more in my happiness and strength daily. I am becoming more of who I want to be versus just what is expected of me and it is very freeing. I love my life.

I found a few great quotes that really sum up everything.

> *"Happiness is letting go of what you think your life is supposed to look like and celebrating it for everything that it is."*
> Mandy Hale, author

> *"Accept no one's definition of your life; define yourself."*
> Robert Frost, author

## STRATEGIES TO UNLOCK YOUR INNER WARRIOR

1. Are you going through the emotions of a daily life or are you truly happy with where you are and who you are?

_____
_____
_____
_____
_____

2. What do you do daily, weekly or monthly to focus on yourself?

_____
_____
_____
_____
_____

3. What can you change or give up that will put you on the path to where you want to go?

_____
_____
_____
_____
_____

4. Are you more concerned with others happiness at the cost of your own? How is this beneficial?

_____
_____
_____
_____
_____

5. Where does your strength come from? Do you know you can be strong and still not have it all together?

_____
_____
_____
_____
_____

6. Do you have a verse or quote you can lean on daily when you are struggling or feeling overwhelmed?

_____
_____
_____
_____
_____

# ABOUT AMANDA POWELL

Amanda Powell is the owner of *The A Team of Keller Williams*. She began her Real Estate career in 2010 in East Texas. After relocating to Maryland in early 2012 Amanda received her Maryland Real Estate license and began working for Long and Foster. Diving into helping families Amanda was awarded Rookie of the Year in 2013 and Agent of the Year in 2014. Since 2013 she has received several designations and completed her Bachelors of Science with a concentration in Marketing in the Fall of 2012.

Amanda specializes in helping Military families relocate to and from all over the world to purchase and sell. Her goal is to make the PCS process as smooth as possible. Helping VA buyers be better prepared for the home purchasing process is important. Amanda also works hard for Sellers with extensive marketing knowledge and aggressive negotiation expertise.

Amanda understands the needs of Military families as she is a military spouse. She has been married to her spouse for sixteen years. Chris has been an active duty Soldier for twenty years. Chris and Amanda have PCS'ed five times over sixteen years. Amanda and Chris have two children, Krystyne and Christopher. In her free time Amanda enjoys the gym and spending time with family and friends.

## CONTACT AMANDA

- Website: www.TheATeamMD.com
- Email: Amanda@TheATeamMD.com
- Phone: 443-818-1299 (mobile)
- Phone: 410-729-7700 (office)

# CHAPTER 11
# ADVERSITY: FRIEND OR FOE OF YOUR INNER WARRIOR

By Edward Reed

The universe has many forces that mold ordinary people into warriors who battle the forces that oppose growth.

Many years ago a young lady was introduced to the powerful force we call adversity in her childhood. The universe molded her into a mighty trainer of warriors. As a young child this woman learned at an early age the importance of resiliency. Without going into too much detail of her private business, trust me when I say her life was no easy road. This woman is my hero, I've learned many important lessons from her past and have benefited from her training for almost fifty years. This woman is my mother. The universe gave her two options in the midst of adversity-give up or overcome.

Adversity can be a friend or foe. Adversity does not discriminate. Regardless if one is wealthy or poor, healthy or unhealthy, wise or foolish, male or female, from one country or another. Adversity comes in many forms: Illness, natural disasters, loss of loved ones, financial hardships, accidents, etc. What separates one person from another is how they choose to respond to adversity. For some adversity is an opportunity to demonstrate strength. For most of us we prefer to keep adversity far away as possible. The reality is it is not if adversity will come, trust me it will show up uninvited.

I will never forget 2017 was on its way to being one of my greatest years. I won various awards, hosting a TV show, building my business, co-writing books, keynote speaking, and I even shared the stage with John Maxwell.

Then one night in September I got a text message followed by series of phone calls that rocked my world. Twenty-four hours prior, I just finished a speaking engagement. In a state of shock and confusion I learned of the untimely and unexpected death of my beloved brother. The following seventy-two hours required me to take charge of mobilizing my family and resources. Adversity bulldozed right into my life in a mighty way. I went from discussing empowerment and community building to talking with funeral homes to make arrangements to get my brother's body. I consoled my parents, brothers, sister-in-law, and cousins. Within two days I escorted my mother and sister-in-law to see my brother for the last time. I kissed his forehead and said goodbye. The next day my brothers and I picked up his remains. With tears coming down my face, I carried what was once a big strong man, in two containers. Holding both containers tightly as if they were fragile babies.

For the next ten months, everything was put on hold. I hit an all-time low. Then on June 4th 2018, adversity paid me another visit. This time in the form of Transient Ischemic Attack (TIA) also known as a mini-stroke. The reality of neglecting my wellness became crystal clear. As I laid in the hospital bed, I embraced my friend Adversity. We had a long heart to heart conversation. Adversity explained, *"I can be your foe or friend, it's all up to how you see me and your response. I can train you to become a warrior or paralyze you with fear. As long as you can breathe, you can be victorious."* We continued our conversation with clear points. The message was, *"To be a warrior first, you need a clear vision for your life anchored in your purpose fueled by your passion. Next, play out the vision with you as the main character of your story. You see each day is a blank page of opportunity field at the end of the day by the decisions you made throughout the day. Understand your beliefs impact your reaction to your thoughts, your thoughts drive your thinking, your thinking is manifested in your actions. So my friend do you believe I am your friend or foe?"* As one who believes in universal laws, I understood we receive what we put out into the universe. I begin to ask myself, how should the next chapter of my life play itself out? While thinking about my response the words of one of my mentors, Paul Martinelli, came to mind. He said, *"If you want your life to change, change the frequency you are tuned into."* Paul was spot-on, my Inner Warrior had become a prisoner of limited beliefs, tuning in to the frequency of being wounded.

My narrative had changed and a piece of me was asleep. The more I began fiddling with the stations of life, my search for the right frequency grew stronger. I looked at the ceiling of my hospital room, started talking with God about my current situation. Years ago I discovered the benefits a building a relationship with God versus getting caught up in religious rituals. I'm not judging anyone's religious practices, for me having a relationship with God and Jesus at the spiritual level has worked best for me even when I'm not at my best. My question to God was, *"Why did adversity come into my life like this, I've spent most of my life helping other people overcome hardships, I've devoted my life to equipping and empowering others, and to be honest I miss my brother and it really hurts! It hurts! It feels like part of me died when he died. I've been strong for everyone and I just don't understand why. Why God, why?"* The next morning the neurologist paid me a visit he said, *"Mr. Reed, your test results look good so we need to talk about the risk factors. Your diet, exercise, sleep, and stress."* I replied, *"I know I need to lose some weight and I'm working on that."* Then my mom, who is my number one hero interjected, *"Edward you never dealt with the death of your brother."* The neurologist looked at me and I replied, *"I don't worry about what I don't control, I'm all right."* He firmly told me, *"If you don't deal with your stress it will find a way to manifests itself through your body."* It was time for me to change the station.

Since my brother's departure from his body, my cousin Theresa and I have grown much closer. She has been a big sister to me and helped me to be still. Her love, wisdom, energy, and spirit nursed my wounded Inner Warrior. Following my mini-stroke, also known as the *"Wake up Call,"* I had a series of doctor appointments with specialists. The message was loud and clear, to reduce the probability of having a full-blown stroke or heart attack, I needed to change. The reality was something was going to change. You see, every reaction has a new reaction. Our choices impact the multiple dimensions of our lives right at the core of our existence - spiritually, physically, and emotionally. Everything that happens at the core level affects everything else we do. We can choose to be victorious or victims to the adversities of life. Adversities don't control your response, they are simply situations you must deal with. To deal with adversity, I have chosen to live my life as in a constant state of evolution. Thus I am committed to continuous growth through learning, loving, and leading. My Inner Warrior has reawakened fueled by my passion to live out my purpose, nursed by the vibrational energy of all those who contributed to the new station I tuned into. Since my *"Wake up Call"* and the anniversary of my brother's departure, I've been blessed to continue to be used by God to help others even more than I did before. New doors have opened, I've returned to conducting seminars, workshops, keynote speaking, mentoring, writing, developing programs, and hosting shows. My Inner Warrior won the battle that has triggered my transformation. In 2018, a tribe came together to start an online wellness and self-

*Transformation starts within!*

care community on Facebook called *Empowerment Wellness Team*. To learn more about the team, search for *Empowerment Wellness Team* in Facebook Groups.

More importantly than me is you. Life can be very interesting when we change how we respond to unfortunate situations that happen in our lives. There's an Inner Warrior inside of you, waiting to be awaken by tuning into a new frequency. Perhaps your Inner Warrior was wounded on the battlefield of life. No matter how bad your wounds maybe, I know one thing for sure, since you are reading or listening to this book you've been given a gift of a new day of life. With this gift is an opportunity to strengthen your Inner Warrior. Adversity can be a friend who demands your attention and prepares you for the next battle or it could be your foe who provides the conditions for you to accept defeat.

Adversity never makes your decisions. It is simply the situation you must have address, and the choice is yours. Here a few actions items and questions to help you along your journey:

## STRATEGIES TO UNLOCK YOUR INNER WARRIOR

1. Write down the biggest challenge that you're facing at this time in your life.

_____
_____
_____

2. Visualize yourself overcoming this challenge. Think about how it feels emotionally, physically and spiritually. Write down or audio record yourself describing this feeling of victory.

_____
_____
_____
_____
_____

3. What resources do you need to use to strengthen your Inner Warrior? Who is nursing your Inner Warrior? Does your library consist of videos, books, podcast, seminars, and workshops to help you move forward?

_____
_____
_____
_____
_____

4. How is the frequency you're tuned into supporting your growth or is it time to change the station?

_____
_____
_____
_____
_____

5. Who in your camp, is depending on your Inner Warrior to be victorious in battle?

_____
_____
_____
_____
_____

6. Who is in your inner circle can help you be your accountability partner to advance forward? Create a check in schedule with your partner establishing a time and date. Schedule it stick to it.

_____
_____
_____
_____
_____

7. Now it's time to write the next few pages of the story that will be the start of the next chapter of your life. Today I made a decision to get stronger, I...

_____
_____
_____
_____
_____
_____

# ABOUT EDWARD REED

After spending over 20 years focusing on developing students and strengthening communities, Ed realized the best way to help future generations was to become an influential leader who impacts those who impact others in the workplace, community, schools, and families. His life mission to transform lives through leadership development, wellness and self-care, and personal growth. As a humble leader, who overcame challenges, setbacks, and other barriers Ed credits his success to his faith, parents, professors, mentors, and coaches for equipping him with the skills and mindset necessary for beating the odds of attaining success.

For more than 25 years, Ed has successfully lead, empowered and coached students, parents, aspiring leaders, professionals, executives, and leadership teams. Ed is an Executive Director with the John C. Maxwell Team were he provides executive coaching, leadership training, and keynotes globally. Driven by his belief that people are the most valuable resources in every organization and that cultivating a culture of leadership is critical to long-term organizational success. His coaching and leadership training focuses on empowering and equipping people to effectively connect with others, stretch beyond their comfort zone, and apply sound wisdom to build their foundation for long-term success. His passion is visible when he is developing leaders of all ages to become creative solution innovators.

## CONTACT EDWARD

- Website: www.JohnMaxwellgroup.com/EdwardReed
- Twitter: www.Twitter.com/EReedSpeaks
- Email: EReed@i5ls.com
- Phone: 301-335-6689

# CHAPTER 12
# PEEL OFF THE LABEL: YOU'RE PRICELESS!

By Samuel Rowland

From the moment I was born: I've had vision problems. But, not "normal" vision problems…I mean "mom-cried-as-the-doctors-told-her-I-was-legally-BLIND-and-would-never-drive-play-sports-or-enlist-in-the-army;" vision problems!

I didn't even know my sight was different from others until I was in my doctor's office at four-years-old being **told** my sight *was* different from others. That's when I started wearing eyeglasses.

At first, it was hard to understand. *Why do I have to wear these uncomfortable things?* I didn't like them! I didn't like how they made me **DIFFERENT**! I got used to them though, and a part of me accepted: *this is how it will be from now on.* ***I have*** *to wear glasses forever!*

But as I thought those things, there was still another part of me saying, *"No! Do NOT bow down to these chaining-shackles!"* At the time, I didn't understand the part of me refusing to accept low vision as a permanency, but now I do:

### It's My <u>Inner Warrior</u>!

You see, God's hand has been on me since *BEFORE* I was born! When mom first learned she was pregnant with me, God said, *"You're going to have a son. His name will be Samuel!"* Then, God began to show her visions of *His* calling upon my life.

One of the visions she constantly speaks of: is me standing before thousands preaching and prophesying as my hands are raised into the air! I'm **NOT** wearing eyeglasses **nor** contacts! My eyes are perfectly healed!!! I hold onto this vision with everything! I know my God **WILL** bring it to pass!

At only four years old, I experienced something AMAZING: my nana took me to Bible school at a local church and as I heard more of Jesus, I realized I needed him;

### *"I Can't Live Without Him!"*

The very moment we arrived home, I told mom I wanted to ask Jesus into my heart! Mom was so excited but asked God if I was too young to understand salvation. When God answered her, his words were very *"stern"* as he replied,

***"Samuel WILL KNOW who I AM! He WILL DO all that I've created him to do! Whether you teach him or not, he WILL STILL KNOW me!"***

Then, she felt God gave her a choice to either be part of my calling or not! (Obviously she agreed, and he showed her she'd be blessed within her choice!)

My quest to learn how to live for Jesus began as I soon learned, even though I was *"saved,"* I didn't understand a lot. *Why is it still hard to see things? Why is my vision not healed? I thought accepting Jesus would make everything perfect immediately, but that's not how salvation works!* Accepting Jesus **GIVES** the **HOPE** that things **WILL** become **BETTER**, become **DIFFERENT** than ever before!

### Salvation isn't a one-time occurrence, it's a lifelong RELATIONSHIP!

As I grew, God continually showed his love, as he brought a wonderful vision specialist to my classroom in 2013; I'm so thankful! She brought special devices (magnifier/desktop acrobat monitor) to help me see my work better!

During this same year, we moved from my grandparent's home into a house of our own! It was exciting to live with just mom, my baby brother, and myself, but it was also weird! I didn't like living without my grandparents because they were a comfort to me, but mom made it fun and we got used to it.

Soon, mom started dating her friend and eventually married him. When we first met, I thought: *Yes! I actually have a dad!* He played games, pushed us on our swing set, and danced silly with us whenever he visited!

In the summer of 2014, my uncle Johnathan became sick. Leading up to his sickness, he'd experienced a few mini heart attacks, but doctors placed a stint into his heart and I was relieved! However, when he got sick that summer, we found out he had cancer. It was scary, but I thought: *if he can beat heart attacks, he can beat anything!*

Over the next two-years, Johnathan spent a lot of time in and out of the hospital. One night, our family visited the emergency room with him and I watched everyone hide tears from their faces while we waited. We stayed late into the evening, as I continued praying: *He can't die, God! He's too young! He can't die, he just can't God!* (And he didn't at that time.)

During that same year, we began attending a new church and I drew closer to God. My Sunday teacher reminded me of a radiant sunflower; **I couldn't look away, she was on fire for God!**

We began our class by dancing to songs (*Speak Life & Move* by *TobyMac*) and worshiping God; I wanted to attend as much as possible! However, a battle was beginning within our family at home, as my parents began to argue over the types of music being played or the movies being watched.

## God showed us: influences like *that* WILL slow growth down with him: they're an INTERFERENCE!

I noticed if I didn't watch or listen to *"that"* stuff (stuff with bad scenes or cussing), I acted more respectful. However, if I watched videos with bad language, I noticed **MY** language would become bad! It **MATTERS** what type of shows watched or music listened to! The more vulgar they are, the less room for God you'll have in your heart!

As I sought God's wisdom during the summer of 2016, I decided to get water baptized at church! All of my family came, including a very-sick Johnathan; him and I had become close over the past two years. Even though he was in a wheel chair, he traveled to church to watch me!

## I was so happy to be baptized because I was ready to accept my calling for Jesus and knew I'd help lead the world to God!

Later that week, as we began to leave my grandparents' home, mom forgot something and quickly ran back inside while my siblings and I waited in our car. As I began to feel scared, I saw an angel standing in front of the car, smiling as it held the Holy Bible; immediately my fear was gone!

## That's the first time I saw an angel, but definitely not the last!

At church one Sunday, towards the end of summer 2016, our preacher asked if anyone needed prayer. Mom asked, *"would you like to have your vision prayed for?"*

*"No, I want to pray for Johnathan to be healed!"* I exclaimed.

At first, she looked shocked, but immediately agreed and walked me to the front of church. When I stood at the front of the line, I told our pastor I was standing in for Johnathan because he was in the hospital again. We prayed for Johnathan like never before and he was released from the hospital the very next evening!

I believe God heard our prayer, touching him with healing as he came home for almost two weeks with renewed energy; he was so happy as he done things he hadn't been able to in months!!!

But then, he got sick again and went back into the hospital. It seemed as though our family fell apart. Suddenly, we stopped going to church and started listening and watching the same type of stuff we had before.

Then, we began fighting bumblebees in our laundry room and wood scorpions in our living room. By August, our hot water heater burst, flooding the entire back side of our home. There was too much damage to fix all at once, so we moved back in with my grandparent's until it could be fixed, or we could find a new house.

> *"I don't understand the battles coming against our family!"*
> **I cried to God!**

Then he showed he was still with me as I started third grade that year and met my teacher. She showed such compassion because she'd had vision problems herself and knew what challenges I faced every day.

My teacher went above and beyond to accommodate my vision and color blindness. Not all teachers I've had were as willing to help as she did; in her class, I was never treated as a burden. I'm so thankful for her kindness!

But…then the unimaginable happened early that December: my Uncle Johnathan passed away.

> **I've never cried so hard in my life…
> I felt like I couldn't breathe, it hurt so bad.**

The grief lasted weeks until God showed me Johnathan wasn't suffering anymore and was in a better place. Then, I was able to *let him go* even though I still missed him immensely. The sadness was no longer unbearable as hope filled my soul, knowing I'll see him again in Heaven!

Just after Christmas that year, we toured a new home that could become ours! It was *SO* nice! God told mom if she walked around the house claiming it, he would give it to us! So, I watched my parents do exactly that and later that night, we found out the bid was accepted, and we got the house! We immediately began moving in as God led us to a new church about forty minutes from our new home!

As 2017 began, our family continued to attend church steadily and life seemed to stabilize. This is when I sought after a more personal relationship with God; I wanted the Holy Ghost!

**I knew the power of speaking in tongues as I watched my mom do it and the moment I got it, I felt unstoppable!!!**

At first, I was nervous praying in tongues, but the more I did it, the stronger I felt the spirit of God growing inside of me! Whenever I didn't know what to pray, I'd pray in the spirit (the Bible says the Holy Spirit prays a perfect prayer!), so, on the night everything changed within my family, I didn't hesitate to pray in tongues!

**God doesn't always answer our prayers as we expect, but he DOES answer them!**

In late April 2017, my parents got into a small argument which led to my dad blaring obscene music from his vehicle. My brother and I were in our room praying for God to stop the arguing, when suddenly we felt the house shake! As my dad had revved his vehicle to leave, he said the throttle stuck causing his vehicle to crash into our porch instead!

I looked out from my window in time to see his wrecked SUV, as he walked down the road cussing the sky. That's the night we found out my dad battled a drug addiction at work that we knew nothing about.

Once dad left, mom packed our bags and took us to my grandparent's for the next week. I didn't know what to think as dad reached out to mom: promising changes, swearing God showed him the gates of hell, and that he'd never touch drugs again.

I told mom, *"Everybody deserves a second chance"* and eventually we went back home. During the next couple of months, life seemed to go smoothly. We continued church and my parents seemed to get along better. Once June approached, I was excited to see my cousins from Alabama. (We only visit during breaks from school throughout the year, so I always look forward to summer break)

We enjoyed time together for a few weeks, then on July 25th, something amazing happened! My family and I were pulling into our driveway late that evening, when I saw an angel standing at the edge of our yard!

**It was an extremely TALL angel, with a white, blazing light radiating from its entire being! It stood in ATTENTION: like as a GUARDIAN!**

It was unlike any angel I've ever seen before! It was much larger with visibly strong muscles and beautiful attire. <u>Its very presence made me feel protected and safe!</u>

*"WOW!"* I exclaimed. *"Do y'all see that?!"* I asked, but no one else saw the **WARRIOR-ANGEL** except me! Unbeknownst to our family, he was there on assignment as the next morning forever

changed our lives.

Mom dropped me off at my first day camp on that next morning, as she finished errands with my younger siblings. Without knowledge of what awaited, she turned onto the blind, uphill beginning of our road without seeing a small child in it. Immediately, she turned her car around and called 911. However, the child was killed instantly, changing mom forever.

Only God knows why that child was in the road that day, but I'm thankful I wasn't in the car with everyone. The pain I witnessed from the accident, I believe would be too hard for most to bare. So, the next few weeks were very hard on our family, but life continued despite mom's heartache.

Before long, school started back, and I entered fourth grade. I couldn't wait for basketball season to start, as I'd shocked my vision doctors when I began playing in second grade and was really good! Our family was welcoming the familiarity of practices and games each week.

**God has blessed me in spite of my eyesight!**
**Playing basketball feels so natural to me!**

None of us had any idea how our lives would change after mom's accident. However, I **felt BIG CHANGES** were coming as God called mom to write a book for him, *"To Mend The Broken."* I watched as she typed endlessly, and a new hope birthed into my heart for the will of God in our lives.

Even though God began to move within my family, the enemy also tried to stop God's plans for us. Once school started back, the bullying started as well. I'd never experienced bullying before, as I'd always been a well-tempered student without enemies, but suddenly I found myself on the receiving end of other kids' ridicules over my mom's accident.

*"Baby-killer!"* They would hiss. *"Your mom's a murderer!"* It hurt so bad, my mom was NOT those things! *"Hey blind boy,"* they'd say as they walked into me, *"can't you see?!"*

It hurt to be taunted, but even worse to watch kids deny what they said before our teachers. I came home every day after school, enraged as I exclaimed, ***"I'm not going back!"*** But the anger would dissolve into hurt as I asked, ***"Why do they hate me so bad?"***

Mom attended countless meetings over the bullying, but nothing changed. Kids continued to say mean statements and eventually adults chimed in sarcastic remarks to me as well.

Once November arrived, I'd had enough of the bullying! So, when a kid on my school bus called me obscene names repeatedly, I reacted and punched him. I thought reacting would make it all stop, but immediately, I felt remorse. When I got home, I asked mom if it would ever stop?

The kid apologized the next day and the taunting seemed to pause for a moment, but, then began again as kids lashed out JUST TO GET A REACTION from me! I began to fight more at school while I sought God's help!

By winter break, I was beyond excited to get away from school and celebrate my **TENTH BIRTHDAY** as my parents surprised me with tickets to my 1st **EVER** UK basketball game at Rupp Arena!

How mom got our tickets was an awesome story! As a local news station heard, the sports anchor loved it and wanted to interview me at the game! My segment was aired on TV across central Kentucky and it was the best birthday ever!!! Through all of the excitement, I was able to forget about the bullying; I was able to forget about the horrible year we just faced.

Once winter break ended, a small group of friends surrounded me at school, asking about being on TV. It was an innocent moment, but some of the other kids overheard us talking and got mad! They told our teacher I was bragging, who in return told me to *not* talk about my birthday present anymore. After that, the same kids told my entire class they weren't going to be my friend, so no one else should be either.

**I was heartbroken. I didn't understand how kids could be so mean! But I learned to: Stay calm, be *proactive* instead of *reactive*, and tell an adult!**

I put this new anti-bullying motto to work and clung to basketball, refusing to allow anything to affect it! If my vision couldn't hinder the enjoyment of my sport, then nothing could! I practiced every day and was excited to be told I was one of the best defensive players in the league. Our team even won the championship!

Even though heartaches continued throughout the remainder of the school year, I held onto my faith: *everything* happens for a reason. I also held onto hope that God **WOULD** fulfill the **Word** he gave me that previous autumn:

> *"Samuel, I'm getting ready to show up and show out within your life and the life of your family in such a way never seen before! You will want for nothing! Your family will want for nothing! Provision will become no object for your family as I show myself in a great and mighty way! Expect it suddenly!"*

Once July came to an end this past year, I felt a stirring in my spirit: ***change*** **was coming to our family!** The entire last week of July, I awoke every day to the sound of God's voice. The first morning God said, *"July 28th. July 28th. Your mother's book. July 28th."* I had no idea what that meant, so I ran downstairs and told mom what God said! Unbeknownst to me, God had given mom a dream the night before which she was also told her book had to be finished by that Saturday, July 28th!

**God was using me to confirm what he'd already showed mom!**

The next morning, I heard God's voice again as I awoke, saying, *"July 28th. Midnight Hour. Midnight. July 28th."* So, I ran downstairs and told mom what God said, not knowing He'd already shown her she needed to prepare for July 28th just as the women in the Bible, so she didn't miss her blessing! (Matthew 25)

For the rest of that week, God gave me one and two word phrases concerning mom's book. Every single day, God used me to confirm what he'd already told her each night before! I didn't understand it then, but:

**God was preparing the WARRIOR inside of me which was placed there before I was even born: TO PROPHESY!**

As July 28th approached, mom finished her book and made a hard copy to deliver to her publisher in North Carolina. However, a tension began to build in our house the night before, as if war was coming.

I wasn't shocked the devil tried to stop mom from leaving that Saturday morning, but I was shocked however, that my dad allowed him to try to do it through him. That morning, Dad got so upset at mom for making the trip that he started screaming obscenities at God repeatedly, then he left. I was heartbroken.

*WHY* would anyone ever say such statements to God?! Who would *WANT* to spend eternity *AWAY* from God?! Mom finished packing quickly and drove me and my siblings to stay with our grandparents' while she was gone, but I felt a peace about it all.

*"You can't let anything stop you,"* I told her. *"You've got to do what God said, no matter what the cost."* She smiled, then held my hand the rest of our drive. *"I love you,"* she said.

Though I was hurt by dad's choices, I knew it was the enemy causing him to make them; all I saw was darkness around him whenever I looked at him. Through dad's words and actions, he willingly invited the enemy to use him, but I'm thankful God shielded us as the enemy tried destroying our family and I asked God to forgive my dad.

**I *knew* something supernatural was happening that weekend! But I had no IDEA he was answering a prayer of mine: to have my story heard!** While mom was in North Carolina, he opened a doorway for **ME** to write within this book! **ME**! A ten year old boy from Kentucky!

**If God can use me, he CAN and WILL USE YOU!!!**

Last week, as we pulled into our driveway, mom asked, *"Samuel do you see any angels tonight?"* At first, I thought no, but then I looked at our front porch and saw an angel! It was big and tall as it stood at the corner of our porch fanning its wings.

*"Let's tell him he's welcome here,"* mom said as we walked into our front yard praising God! I began to see multiple angels!

*"Samuel, did you know when one prays, they command 1,000 angels to flight, but when two or more people pray, they command 10,000 angels to flight?"* Mom asked.

*"No,"* I replied, as we held our hands into the air praying for guardian angels to place a hedge around our family. As we held hands and prayed in tongues, I literally felt the ground begin to shake!!!

**It was as if a nuclear bomb of God's bright light exploded in our front yard, driving hundreds of demons from the ground and I could see strongholds shattered into billions of pieces!!!**

Now, here I am in August, sharing my story to spread encouragement! No matter what you're going through: whether bullying, a heartbreaking accident, a death in your family, or loving someone with an addiction…know **God is there!** God will never leave you nor let you down! **Whenever you're scared, call upon the name of JESUS! All of hell will tremble!**

### STRATEGIES TO UNLOCK YOUR INNER WARRIOR

1. Have you been told you have a medical condition? How did you feel about being seen as *"DIFFERENT"*?

_____
_____
_____
_____
_____

2. Did you know God calls us as Christians **TO BE DIFFERENT?** (1 Peter 2:9) He LOVES our differences! How can you change your thoughts to embrace your differences?

_____
_____
_____

3. Have you ever been bullied? Have you ever bullied someone else? How did that make you feel? How does God want us to handle bullying?

_____

_____

_____

_____

4. Have you heard God talk to you? Whether inside of your head or as an actual voice? How did it make you feel? If not, you can ask God to help you hear his voice more clearly! Write your answers and pray to God here:

_____

_____

_____

_____

5. Did you know that it MATTERS what type of music you listen to or shows you watch? What steps can you take to filter the influences your eyes see and your ears hear?

_____

_____

_____

_____

5. Have you ever known someone who battled with influences such as alcohol or drugs? How did that make you feel? Jesus CAN set people free from that! How can you pray for that person? Write your prayer here!

_____
_____
_____
_____
_____

If you've never accepted Jesus into your heart, there's no better time than right now! Pray this prayer with me and then reach out to me to let me know you did! I'll welcome you to the hope I know in Jesus!

*"Lord, Jesus, I believe you died on the cross and shed your blood for me! I believe that you are the one TRUE SAVIOR and I ask you into my heart to live forever! Please forgive me of all of my sins and help me live a life pleasing to you. In Jesus name, I ask. AMEN!"*

# ABOUT SAMUEL ROWLAND

Samuel is a student within the state of Kentucky. He lives with his parents and younger siblings. He accepted Jesus as his personal savior at 4 years old and was baptized with the Holy Ghost at 9 years old! He has begun cultivating his gift of prophesy and supernatural eyesight, which he believes God will use throughout his life to bless others!

Aside from Samuel's faith, he is extremely athletic, playing most sports, but his heart beats for basketball! He is also considering joining MMA and Track!

Samuel is tremendously talented in his school studies, as he scores within the top percentile of his class each year. He has also been an avid member of the academic team for the past three years, as well as a participant of the prestigious Duke University Talent Identification Program!

> *"I've only seen the launch of the **Warrior** God has placed within me! I plan to seek God and stand **bolder in my faith** than ever before! **NEVER** give up on who **YOU** are! I hope my words reach the ends of this world to save people from a life of hopelessness! There is a **warrior** in all of us, no matter how old we are!"*

Special thanks & recognition:
My Parents. My Nana & Papaw, Nat, Ethan, Ally, Mrs. Rita, Mrs. Peavie, and Mrs. Noe!

## CONTACT SAMUEL

- Facebook: www.Facebook.com/AuthorSamuelRowland
- Email: BlessedPierce@icloud.com

# CHAPTER 13
# EVICT THE VICTIM, EMBRACE THE VICTOR!
By Aarti Royan

**"How would you like your coffee mam?" Screamed the barista!**

I gazed at her not even realizing I was at a café and was ordering a coffee...and I can assure you that I was not having an out of body experience!!!

*"Well, umm, umm, I'll have a …. …I am not sure"* was my response. Much to the disgust of not just the barista, but the long line of 'busy' people behind me, I walked away, disappointed in myself.

This was in the winter of 2008 shortly after a Pressure cooker blew up in the kitchen and left my right arm scarred for life, from first degree burns. This accident, I must admit, was only the icing on the cake, as far as life pressures go.

I was inundated with stress and experiencing mild to borderline depression occurring from all sources, particularly parenting a teenager and a toddler at the same time, as well as just being discontent about my lack of purpose and direction in life and from carrying tremendous regret and guilt from my past. All this, while I was enjoying a seemingly successful career and being a top performer at work!

In mid 2009, my depression began to progress in more ways than I had welcomed. I was becoming quite the walking/talking zombie who was drifting away like a log! It is during such times that trials, pain, and suffering seem to all compound or perhaps magnify themselves, at the slightest opportunity. That overwhelming feeling... Is all this really happening to me?

*Who am I?*

*What am I doing here?*

*Why did I do the things I did?*

*Why is my life not as normal as others?*

*What is going on?*

*My future looks hazy, I hardly have hope!*

The above thoughts were often followed by anxiety. Anxiety was a frequent visitor who used to make an appearance quite significantly and conjure up equations in my mind that made two plus two appear like ten!

During this season, I was also not feeling the best physiologically. I was overweight by about fifty pounds and rather unhealthy and unfit which I am sure contributed in more ways, than I can imagine, to my mental and emotional state.

That coffee episode was just one of the many occasions that made me realize, that I was simply existing in my nomadic land.

Juggling a busy career life and some tough family circumstances, while feeling overwhelmed, hopeless empty, and discontent on the inside, drove me to a point where I had even contemplated suicide.

However, thinking back now, I realize it was that tiny insular world I was living in also known as the mind. I was living 24/7 within the confines of my mind. I was processing and acting on thought patterns and belief systems that were formed based on my life experiences, my conditioning, and the way I was nurtured and socialized. I chose to wear a dark lens that had very limited perspective.

I created the problems, I analyzed my problems, and to top it all – I felt terribly sorry for my problems and found comfort in self-loathing. I was Aarti, the VICTIM. Head down, droopy shoulders, and not happy with myself or with others around me.

April 2009, welcome rock bottom! Everything, everything was going wrong. My anxiety attacks increased dramatically. I kept awake most nights worrying about the future and where I was heading. I was making decisions based on my past...

Something had to change.

God had other plans.

I started desperately seeking for the answers for all the big life questions and went on a hard-core exploring journey. I researched various worldviews and went through hours and hours of various schools of philosophy and spirituality. Surely someone, somewhere had to know if there was a way I could come to terms with my past. A past that included hurting my parents and siblings through my rebellion, being a very young mum, and raising my kids in the best way I knew possible and the list goes on...

**Interestingly, in all my years of growing up I did have a 'religious' foundation but was completely devoid of an authentic spiritual connection.**

My quest took me to a local church and I found myself enrolling in an Alpha Course, which is a ten week course that helps explore the meaning of life.

I started to find the answers to life's biggest questions – the pennies began to drop.

This course really addressed my skepticism and solidified my beliefs both in an intellectual, historical, and spiritual capacity. I found my answers in Jesus and committed my life to Christ in a real and personal way.

I always knew that Jesus was God but had never clearly discerned the difference between a religious or superstitious belief to experiencing a personal relationship with God Himself.

The moment I had embraced this truth and made a choice to commit my life to Jesus as my Lord and Savior, a huge shift occurred. I was starting to see hope and light at the end of my tunnel.

However, I still had to deal with Aarti the victim! She had been part of me for all my life but the apparent discontent with her was what led me to find the absolute truth.

One of the first things I had to do was to sincerely repent of living the life I was living. That is a life that was dictated by my whims and fancies, my thoughts and feelings, and to evict Ms. Victim.

Thanks to the support of a great church I had begun to face some of these goliaths, head on.

I went on to do a twelve month discipleship course, called *"Growing to Maturity"* that helped transform my entire being. I was no longer an avid seeker turned believer, but I was a believer on my way to becoming a disciple.

**This was it – The moment that I knew
I had to go into battle with the victim in me.**

A weekend away, called the *"Freedom weekend,"* gave me the perfect opportunity to deal with my baggage and my victim mind-set. It was a funeral of sorts- I had to bury the old man (or rather the old woman), the old me in her entirety! I had to call out regret, self-pity, guilt, shame, condemnation, deception, and many other badges for who they were and break ties with each of them.

## Jesus deals with the Victim mindset:

In John 5: 5-8, we read about the healing at Bethesda:

*"Now there was a man who had been disabled for thirty-eight years lying among the multitude of the sick. When Jesus saw him lying there, he knew that the man had been crippled for a long time. So Jesus said to him,* **'Do you truly long to be healed?'**

*The sick man answered him, 'Sir, there's no way I can get healed, for I have no one who will lower me into the water when the angel comes. As soon as I try to crawl to the edge of the pool, someone else jumps in ahead of me.'*

*Then Jesus said to him,* **'Stand up! Pick up your sleeping mat and you will walk!'** *Immediately he stood up—he was healed! So he rolled up his mat and walked again! Now this miracle took place on the Jewish Sabbath."*

I love how Jesus asks the sick man, *"Do you truly long to be healed?"*

The victim in the sick man responds with all the reasons and excuses about why he was unable to be healed. Jesus firmly addresses the sick man and instructs him to pick up his *"SLEEPING MAT"* and walk!

I relate to that sick man at many levels. If I had banked a penny for every excuse I had made, I would be a millionaire!

But Jesus dealt with the sick man in a firm yet loving manner. Firstly, he asked the sick man if he 'Truly' wanted to be healed.

I had to apply that to myself - how earnest was I in **wanting** to be healed? Was I truly at the end of my old self and done with being physically, emotionally, and spiritually sick?

And if I was to follow Jesus' instruction to the sick man, I too had to pick up my sleeping mat, break allegiance with my excuses and self–pity and walk.

But how did I do it? How could I do it? How do I unlock my Inner Warrior and how can I continue doing so?

**The keys to my Inner Warrior lie in my faith, based on understanding. It is the activating of my faith through an understanding that comes from reading and applying the truth of God's word.**

Jesus has promised me in His word; *"But I have come to give you everything in abundance, more than you expect—life in its fullness until you overflow!"* John 10:10 TPT

It is this truth that I needed to grasp in the core of my being. The enemy of my soul on the other hand comes to steal, kill, and destroy.

It was the enemy that had me locked up in victim mode but Christ was now in my life embracing me to be a Victor in Him.

I now had the keys to begin unlocking the Inner Warrior. Dare I say that this warrior/this new creation has surprised herself in more ways than she ever thought possible!

**It is not a genie in a bottle or an instant mantra that just magically makes everything bright and shiny again! Rather it is a daily process of spending time with God in prayer and worship, reading His word, receiving a personal revelation, and acting on it.**

Fundamentally for me, it was a process of receiving God's love and forgiveness and walking in my new identity - This is the essence of a warrior spirit. To understand in his/her heart that he or she is truly and unconditionally loved, fully forgiven, and derives identity from Christ.

It is knowing that I can't change my past or avoid some of the consequences that naturally occur from my past choices but rather in how I choose to respond to them.

Even though I didn't experience miraculous breakthroughs in all of my life circumstances, I had the will and the keys to respond with a warrior spirit. I had a choice to not be a defeatist but in everything to choose to pray and let my petitions be made known to God and trust that He would bring me the breakthrough I needed, at just the right time. God has not failed me!

I love the saying, *"God loves me so much, he loves me just the way I am but God loves me too much to leave me the way I am."*

Once I started to change my perspective and live life through the lens of my Inner Warrior, I started to put my beliefs into action.

My calls to action were in all areas of my life.

I knew something had to change with my health. I made a commitment to take my health serious. How could I be a warrior and live on purpose, if I was lacking energy and feeling tired all the time?

I chose to take the perseverant route. I knew that shortcuts don't work and they are hardly sustainable! Warriors don't choose fast food or microwave methods. We choose to conquer by overcoming with persistence.

The strategy I applied for my health was to eat clean and exercise consistently. I eliminated all the junk from my pantry and chose a clean eating lifestyle. This was not easy. I had to put up a fight, I had to fight those cravings but I could do that because I was now a warrior and not a victim (I don't know of many people who desperately crave steamed vegetables and grilled fish!).

### Discipline and perseverance pay high dividends.

I started to not just lose weight but my energy levels were uncontainable! I had to remind myself that it was the same me who was walking around with no direction or purpose in a pathetic depressed state just a few years prior!

My exercise routines and fitness started to become consistent. I enjoyed the outdoors, taking up cycling, and running. A few years later I took part in a 100Km ultra marathon, go figure!

It was possible! I could be a renewed being.

At this stage my purpose and calling started to become a little more evident. I enrolled in Bible College and went on to complete an associate degree in Theology and Ministry.

I share this not to brag or impress you but to testify that this would never have been possible if I continued living in my spiritually and physically dead self!

Not only did I stop living the victim but I now started to look around and see so many others live like the old me! I grew passionate about helping people who are experiencing the struggles that I did!

### I went from being *"Victim on the mat to Warrior on Mission,"* a transformation that can only be brought by Jesus!

My passion for wellness grew as did my awareness on personal growth and leadership. We have to be able to lead ourselves first in order to help others.

This was my time to unlock my purpose and calling.

I went on to equip myself through further study in personal growth and leadership as well as in my health and wellness journey.

Juggling a full time family and job, part time study and ministry, and working on a business was all starting to become more than possible. I sometimes look back and cannot even believe that this "I" was aimlessly walking to the café, even unsure of the coffee I wanted!

Again, I would be kidding myself if I tell you that my circumstances and problems changed overnight. Quite on the contrary, in some ways the trials even increased but God comes through with a breakthrough, when we are faithful and steadfast.

Warriors on Mission thrive through obstacles. We are robust even in the struggles because our identity and authority, both come from Christ. My warrior choices helped me overcome struggles one by one by choosing to fight with my shield of faith.

From the very moment I decided to pick up my sleeping mat and walk (at that freedom weekend) to where I am now, is nothing short of a miracle. I acknowledge that I have a long way to go and I am certainly not any less of a work in progress, but I celebrate knowing where I was once was to where I am now!

I am hopeful of my future and I know that God is a redeeming and restoring God. God has already immensely done a great work in me and will continue to bring purpose and beauty of my brokenness and ashes.

**There are times that I help people from a place of strength but there are also times that I help and minister from a place of hurt and brokenness. It does not matter. I am a victor either way and will continue to bring people out of 'their mats'!**

What matters is that I continue to feel and experience God's love and intimacy in relationship with Him.

What matters is that my faith is based on an understanding and not out of belief in a formula or a theory.

What matters is that I am spiritually, emotionally, and physically alive now and will continue to be a warrior on mission.

## STRATEGIES TO UNLOCK YOUR INNER WARRIOR

1. Do you know Jesus as your Lord and Savior? Have you committed your life to Him through a faith that comes from understanding?

_____
_____
_____
_____
_____


2. How do you see yourself today? Do you have one or more sleeping mats that you need to get rid of? Are you able to call them out and make a choice to break allegiance to them?

_____
_____
_____
_____
_____

3. Do you feel like a victim who is living out of guilt or shame from the regrets or consequences of your past choices? What are some of them? Are you willing to accept and apply God's forgiveness on each of these areas?

_____
_____
_____
_____
_____

4. How are you doing physically? Do you need to be honest with yourself about the state of your health? Write down 1-3 health goals that you could incorporate into your life immediately.

_____
_____
_____
_____
_____

5. Do you see yourself as the warrior on mission or the victim on the mat? How will YOU start living like the warrior on mission?

_____
_____
_____
_____
_____

# ABOUT AARTI ROYAN

Aarti Royan was born in India and now calls the most livable city, Melbourne, Australia home.

Aarti loves Jesus and her family and is passionate about her faith, writing, and speaking. She is author of a clean eating cook book, *Going Paleo the Indian* way and is also a blogger who writes on spirituality and wellness.

Aarti is a dynamic personality, a great communicator, a wellness and mind coach who believes in the transforming power of Jesus.

An inspirational speaker, Aarti has overcome many of life's obstacles and lives out of her purpose to empower and encourage others to pursue their Mission.

## CONTACT AARTI

- Website: www.JohnCMaxwellGroup.com/AartiRoyan
- Website: www.RobustPrincess.wordpress.com
- Facebook: www.Facebook.com/PaleoToGo.online
- Email: RoyanAarti@gmail.com

## CHAPTER 14
# (YAAW) YOU ARE A WARRIOR
By Carlos E. Vargas

In today's culture we use words and sometimes we don't understand their meaning.

You can see people talking about how to be a warrior. How to beat the competition by being a warrior. We use phrases as 120% or *"I Am All In."* We tell others that we are warriors but what are we really talking about? Have you ever taken the time to think what is a warrior and how it relates to you and what you do on a day to day basis?

One of my favorite philosophers describes a warrior in the following way. *"I have fought the good fight, I have finished the race, I have kept the faith."* (2 Timothy 4:7). Canadian writer and motivational speaker Robin Sharma quotes, *"Be a warrior when it comes to delivering on your ambitions; a saint when it comes to treating people with respect, modeling generosity, and showing up with outright love."*

If we look at trusted sources of knowledge they have different definitions for the word warrior. After years of working thru this idea for my own growth, I have formulated my own definition. For me, a warrior is a brave or experienced soldier, fighter, professional, or person that possesses a heroic or brave mindset and an ethical impulse to follow a different path, which focuses on individual transformation and is on a constant practice to compassionately help others with his gifts, wisdom or knowledge.

Over the years I have found that there are six different areas or buckets from where a warrior draws its strength to keep on going to achieve his goals and deliver his purpose. When you learn to master these areas, you will have success in your personal, professional, and spiritual life. I have experienced it and, in this chapter, I will share my experience on how to release the warrior that is within you.

Mastering any one of the six areas on its own will help you grow, but in my opinion, it will not make you a warrior. Learning to build a lifestyle and working towards applying all of them will help you release the warrior that is within you.

These six areas are Physical Strength, Mental Toughness, Character Development, Emotional Stability, Financial Freedom, and Spiritual Maturity. I will discuss three of these six areas in this chapter.

The first time I heard the word warrior it was a very long time ago. I was about 7 or 8 years old and as many young boys, wrestling was one of the sports I could watch at home and then go and play with my friends. We would jump up and down. I imagined drop kicking my friends and fighting thru the air; landing and flighting elbow on my friends. It was just like the wrestlers used to do.

Then a new wrestler appeared in the show. The Ultimate Warrior. Who was this guy? He had long hair, his face was always painted like a hawk or eagle and was always helping others. He only fought if it was really necessary but immediately became the favorite of everyone. For years he was the favorite for his values and what he represented.

Even after he passed away his character lives on in the hall of fame and is still alive on the current wrestling video games.

From an early age, I start forming my warrior mindset and realizing that inside me there was something different. Like the Ultimate Warrior, there were different situations that helped me to understand that I had been created to be different. With my strength and weaknesses, all of them will help me to become the man I am today and the one that will help others reach their potential.

# The Warriors Physical Strength

Physical Strength is the first area that we normally see in a person. When we look at someone the first thing we notice is their outside physical body. Napoleon Hill once said, *"Strength and growth come only through continuous effort and struggle."*

The idea of having physical strength is something we know and understand but most of the time we don't make the effort to do what is needed. As a kid, I was a healthy kid. I was always told by my mom and those around me. It was really interesting that even so I was told that I was healthy, I was not able to be athletic or play for a long time. My level of energy used to be limited. When playing hide and seek I was caught easily while my friends were still running or hiding on top of a house. The behavior stayed with me all the way until adulthood. Thinking that I was healthy, even though my doctor exams and laboratories showed I was a good health, my waist was climbing to an out of proportion with my mental picture of health. I got to be over 320 lbs.

It got to a point that I had to decide, *will I stand by what some people say, or will I take control and build my physical strength*. My dear friend, it's not been easy. But after the last ten years of this new journey, I can report that I am in one of the best shape seasons of my life. It all started with a decision to build my physical strength.

A warrior needs to understand that his body is what holds him. Without a body, you can't do what you want or need. Arnold Schwarzenegger understood that idea. As a kid, he was not the strongest, but his mind had a determination and goals to reach. The warrior within him wanted to reach those goals and he needed to work on his body to build it to sustain those goals. In the movie *Pumping Iron*, Arnold shows how his determination helps him to build his physical body to reach his goals. He not only reaches his physical body goals but also his business and personal goals.

Does this mean that to be a warrior we all have to be like Arnold? You don't have to become a professional bodybuilder, but you have to build your body. As a warrior, your key is to take care of your body because it is with you for your entire life. To simplify the idea: *"…Your body is the temple of the Holy Spirit"* and if you want him to live inside you, your physical body needs to be in shape. When we start taking care of our body everything else flows. Don't miss this point. I am not saying that you need to be in perfect shape, but on a journey taking care of your body. Learning to make the right decisions that will strengthen your body. When you do this the warrior that is within you will start to take shape and you will be able to withstand what comes your way.

## The Warrior Mental Toughness

As a warrior develops, he also needs to learn to develop his mind. Across the years there have been many different moments where my mindset helped endure and thrive through situations. If you think back to different moments in your life, you will discover it was the way you thought about the situation. It was what helped you accomplish the goal or get through the other side. It was not until you made a clear, concise mental picture of where you wanted to go or needed to get to that made it happen.

When I think of a Warrior I think of a story of a Military commander. He arrived by boat to land at the shores to fight against the enemy. His fellow army men were ready to fight against their opponent. But as a warrior, he wanted to be sure that there would not be anything that would stop them from giving every bit of themselves to fight. He gave them a little pep talk on how much he trusted them. Then he did something that nobody was expecting him to do. He made a decision to burn the boats. He told his army that there was not an option for retreat as now the boats were not accessible to escape to.

If that was one of us, we may have said, *"Oh no! I need a 'plan B' or a backup plan in case this does not work!"* This Military commander was ready to give it his all. I believe that in his mental toughness, he was mentally ready to face what everyone of us will face at some journey in our lives. I learned a lot from this story.

**We must be ready to do whatever it takes to reach the goal that we have is a key characteristic of a warrior.**

We see in the movies or in literature the warrior or hero who always gets to his destiny, no matter the situation. He arrives because his mindset is clear, and he knows that keeping a clear mind is key to maintaining his focus. We need to maintain a clear mind from all things that can distract us from reaching our goal.

*What have you been dreaming about?*

*What is your desire and where you want to go?*

*Do you know how to get there?*

*Are you willing to go the extra mile to get what is yours?*

This and many more questions go thru a warrior mentality in order to prepare for his journey. But they don't think about it with the same mind. The true warrior has transformed their mind. "... **Transform your understanding so you can do what is good and noble"** (Romans 12:1-2)

This mental toughness has helped me to go through difficult times at work and at home; to understand that my Lord will provide everything that I need. He has a purpose for you and me. When I finally understood this all the other things started to flow. My purpose started to become a reality. But it was not until my mind aligned with God's spirit that I was able to move forward.

## The Warrior Spiritual Character Development

In 2014 I was invited to be part of a special event where a group of Leaders from Latin America met in Atlanta, Georgia. During the event there where many great leaders and speakers. My friend and mentor shared the following statement, *"Character is who you are. Reputation is who people think you are. I know for a fact that I have a reputation. That's who people think I am. But I also know that inside of me is my character; who I really am. What I strive for, and I want to say…this is not easy for me, and it's not going to be easy for you, but what I strive to be and do is this: I strive to be bigger on the inside than on the outside."* - John C. Maxwell

A warrior must develop their spiritual character and it must be intentional.

As a warrior, it is important to understand that you will face difficulties. Those difficulties may come in different ways, shapes, and sizes. After I understood this detail, then I was able to understand how to fight the good fight. We face spiritual battles; those can represent themselves in the spiritual realm and also on the physical world.

In the New Testament, Paul instructs Timothy that if he builds his spiritual character fighting the good fight, he will enjoy eternal life. The only way to develop character is to practice. That is the reason why Paul instructed Timothy to practice. (1 Timothy 6:12)

Each warrior in history had some tools. The Samurai had his clothing, armor, and katanas. The Knights from the Round Table had an armor that fit them and helps them be protected. And the Christian Warrior is no exception. We have an armor that is not to be used only when we have problems. It is to be used all the time. We grow by utilizing our gifts.

Our armor is described in Ephesians 6:10-12 and it is to protect us and help us go out and act. Without action, an armor is useless. The apostle Paul said, *"We will use the armor to resist the attacks from our enemy."* Why will the enemy attack you if you are not moving or are a threat to him? The only way you get attacked is when you are moving in closer to your God given purpose. That is the purpose of developing your spiritual character. To be a warrior you must work to fulfill your God given potential in the world. It has nothing to do with a church or with an organization. You and I have been placed on this earth to fulfill our purpose given by God.

So, how do we develop our spiritual character? There are ten principles I have learned over the years that will help you develop your spiritual character.

1. **Maintain Hope** that you will be victorious. It does not matter what we see right now, our hope is in Christ. (1 Thessalonians 5:8)

2. **Maintain A Pure Heart.** As a warrior, our motives cannot get cloudy by what is around us. Our enemy may play some dirty tricks but we must be different. (2 Corinthians 6:4-7)

3. **Stand In Truth.** A true spiritual warrior understands that he is not alone. We have to understand that God already won the battle even before we start it, we belong to God, and the one that is in us is more powerful than the one that is in fighting against us from the world. Our help comes from him, not from us. There is nothing we can do physically that will help us in a spiritual battle. A true warrior knows that his battle strength comes from above. You are not fighting alone! (1 John 4:4)

4. **Develop A Worship Mindset.** A true spiritual warrior understands and knows that his success in battle and in business is directly related to his worship of our heavenly father. This

worship is not only when everything is going good but also in times of need. That is why the Psalmist said it best: *"... he is our help in time of needs."* (Psalms 22:1-4)

5. **Your Needs Will Be Met By Him.** We all have needs and as a warrior we may be helping others, doing things that may require more of us. And sometimes we may think about what will happen with my needs? When will they be met? A spiritual warrior knows and shares with others his trust in that all his needs will be met no matter how big or small they are. (Psalm 138:7)

6. **Come From Victory.** The power to win the battle is not yours. God has all the power to help and destroy what comes our way and as a warrior, I need to learn it, understand it and believe it. (2 Chronicles 25:8)

7. **He is the Lord**, the God of every living thing, there is nothing impossible for him. (Jeremiah 32:27)

8. **We have received authority.** The authority given to me is what I will use to be different and fight the good fight. When I understand the authority given to me, there is nothing impossible for me or YOU. (Matthew 28:18)

9. **Jesus Gives The Spiritual Strength.** My Spiritual strength is not mine it comes from Jesus. As a true warrior that you are you need to learn, where does your strength come from? Philippians 4:13 is my favorite verse of the Bible *"I can do all things in Christ Jesus."*

10. **Press Forward.** When I am tired, I will continue because God will give me the strength. When we get tired, we need to understand and believe that *"He"* will give us the strength. Our weakness is not an excuse for not keep on going. We need to

continue and He will get us to our destination. Our God will help us as he says in Isaiah 40:29.

The Inner Warrior that God has given you is like a lamp. When you purchase a lamp, it will have the description on the box but it does not function as a lamp at this moment. It won't work as long as it stays in the box from the store that it is from. You need to take it out and put it together. Even when you put it together, you still can't do anything with it. You need to plug it into the source of power. You need to plug in the lamp into the electrical outlet in order for that lamp to turn on and shine. But that lamp can shine a little bit or a lot. It depends on the light bulb that we put with it. If we put a 100W LED light bulb it will be a very different story from a 100W regular bulb. Both of them will use the same source of power but the difference will be in the output of the light.

God owns everything. He creates it. He gave it to us. He can take it away and He will also give you something better. (Job 41:11)

Job was a man and he was a warrior. He would wake up in the morning and pray for his family even though he did not know if they had sinned or not. He did it anyway. He took care of those around him and worked hard.

If we look at what the Bible describes of his possessions, he had more than twenty million dollars in equipment (sheep, camels, donkeys, bulls, etc.). This was without counting the people and land needed to have all this equipment. And then he lost it all on a blink of an eye. If the story stopped there, there will not be too much to learn from him, but the story tells us, that he kept on being a warrior, looking towards God and trying to understand what happened.

His friends tried to help and then blamed him for everything that happened, but he kept looking and trying to go to God. In the end,

God showed him that He was his strength and that no matter what happens he will be ok. We see in the last chapter of the book of Job that God was his strength. Everything that he lost he gained it back and was blessed beyond measure. God is all powerful and there is nothing he can't do.

> *"Courage, above all things, is the first quality of a warrior."*
> **Carl von Clausewitz**

You are a warrior. I know that is true. Do you want to know why? The first thing you did was you bought this book. And not only you purchased it. You opened it and you are all the way to the end of this chapter. That tells me that you are a person that is willing to invest in yourself and that are looking to fulfill your God given potential and calling. Your courage to keep on going will move you to new heights.

Don't try to live your life alone. The word warrior is not a synonym for Lone Ranger. When we are experiencing life, we see many things happening around us, but we need to be awake to be able to see those things. Our enemy is always plotting against us. As a warrior, one thing that I need to have present is that I am not alone. If I try to live life alone I will lose.

The word says in Psalm 34:7 that **"The Lord's Angel is around those who fear him and he rescues them."** Theologians agreed that this means that God himself watches over us like Jacob who fought with *"The Angel of the Lord"* and his walk changed. The Almighty God is watching over us.

> *"There are no contests in the Art of Peace. A true warrior is invincible because he or she contests with nothing. The defeat means to defeat the mind of contention that we harbor within."*
> **Morihei Ueshiba**

Do not allow your enemy to defeat you. Release the warrior that is within you. Be the warrior you have been called to be by developing, growing, and exercising the gifts given to you. You will be amazed at how many people will come to see you if you set yourself on fire. So, fill yourself of the Holy Spirit and the world will come to see you burn.

Living to Serve, Lead and to be a Technical Geek.

### STRATEGIES TO UNLOCK YOUR INNER WARRIOR

1. What have you learned about yourself reading this chapter?

___

2. How could you build yourself physically, mentally, and physically to become stronger?

___

3. What realization have you had in knowing what you must commit to in the relationship with yourself and also with God?

___
___
___
___
___

# ABOUT CARLOS E. VARGAS

Living to Serve, Lead and to be a Technical Geek.

For the last twenty years, Carlos Vargas has impacted people's live through his speaking, teaching, and inspiring individuals across Brazil, Mexico, Dominican Republic, Paraguay, Cuba, Puerto Rico, United States, and Europe. Carlos loves being a Transformation agent for people who have current limiting beliefs in their business, personal and spiritual lives. This is the fuel which keep him going.

Carlos works with individual, family, groups, and businesses to help them reduce stress and enjoy life, thru great interaction via their personality and individual leadership competencies.

Carlos Vargas earn his education in the Defenders of the Faith Theological Institute in Santurce, Puerto Rico and later received over than eighty IT certifications during his successful career as an International Architect with different fortune 100 and 500 companies.

Carlos was part of a Elite team of world changers who were invited to travel to Paraguay and help transform the lives of 17,000 people.

As International Leadership and Life Coach, he finished a Tour through the beautiful countries of Brazil and Cuba where he helps countless people to transform their limiting beliefs into new opportunities.

## CONTACT CARLOS

- Website: www.CarlosVargas.com
- Facebook: www.Facebook.com/CarlosEVargasVIP
- Twitter: www.Twitter.com/CarlosVargasVIP
- Instagram: www.Instagram.com/CarlosEVargasVIP

# CHAPTER 15
# THE BIRTHING OF A WARRIOR
By Taffiney Nolan Williams

# The value and purpose of a creation can only be determined by the creator.

Have you ever been at a yard sale and picked up an item, its' package torn, no price tag, or instructions and thought, *"What is this used for?"* Or *"how much is this worth?"* Maybe you thought *"What on earth do you call this thing?"* The purpose, value, and name were unknown because it was separated from the source of the answers to these questions. There was nothing available to determine its' identity. You may ask the salesperson only to be told, *"I don't know but I have used it to.....and I call it.....and I will take.....dollars, and it's yours."*

Tools are the best example of this. I remember the first time I saw a rachet. I had only seen it used as a manner to hammer a nail into the wall and thrown into a pile of other tools. The 1st time I saw my grandfather use it in conjunction with different size sockets to repair a car that he then sold, I realized, this rachet had significant value. Its' value wasn't revealed until it's purpose was exposed based on its' identity.

I've also heard countless stories of antiques being sold for pennies only to realize they're worth millions. The value could not be determined because there wasn't a name on a painting and it was separated from the artist, the creator. However, once the painting was identified with the artist and named, its' true value was placed on it.

In the beginning, Adam was given the task of naming all things created by God. In direct relationship and constant communication with the Creator, he named everything from a pure, undefiled place. God decided that he needed a helper to complement him and once created she was brought to him to name. The man named her woman because she was created from his rib making her a part of him. He named her based on her identity, she was bone of his bone. She was created by God from a part of Adam. God created Adam and Eve with purpose which was clear until they were separated from the Creator through sin.

My question to you now is, *"Who have you allowed to name you?"*

Many years ago, I was faced with a daunting decision.

On a dreary day in October of 1993, the call came from Marie, *"You have to leave town as soon as possible. Lee told me to get my black dress ready because when he finds you, he's going to put a bullet in your head!"*

*'Wow, he's going to take it this far. seven months pregnant with his child and he's really going to kill me. Why should I be surprised? I should have expected this after having him hold a gun to my head seven months prior.'* I knew the day would come when I would have to leave, I just thought I had more time.

See, six months prior, I began implementing my exit strategy. The first step was reaching out to my estranged husband, ML, to come get the oldest two children. The next step was going to a battered-women shelter where I could be safe, get counseling, and help to acquire a place of my own so my babies could come back home. During the intake at the shelter, I found out that I was expecting my 4th child at the age of twenty-two. I was angry, hurt, confused, and scared. Thoughts were racing through my head; *"Now you can never get away from him."*

*"He's going to find you."*

*"You will never be safe."*

All the thoughts appeared to be coming true as he was now calling Marie with threats.

Once the shock of this disturbing message from Marie began to subside, my analytical thinking kicked into high gear. *'I must go home, pack our things, and leave the state. But, where will I go?'* As I was processing and speaking my thoughts aloud, Marie made it clear that she didn't think it was a good idea to go to my house, but I refused to listen. I took the baby to her place and headed to my own. As I put my key into the lock to open the door, the entire door fell inward. He had removed the hinges and propped the door back as if it were okay. He'd found me! I alerted my neighbor who graciously agreed to go in with me. We found that all our clothes were gone. He had taken everything. The house had been ransacked, the babies medicine and breathing machine were gone. The dresser drawers were all over the room, closets emptied, food dumped over the kitchen, and cabinets emptied. Broken glass and trash litter the entire place. He'd found me!

Fear began to rise up inside me. After expressing the situation to my estranged husband ML, I informed him that I was coming to get the kids and we would be going West where my family could help me. He said, *"I'm sorry I placed you in this situation, come back to me and we will work things out, you are my wife."* So, seven months pregnant, an asthmatic baby that had just turned 1 years old, in a five-speed Ford Escort with literally the clothes on our backs, we set out down the highway to the promise of *"let's start over"* once again.

Just a short eighteen months prior, I, ML and our two children migrated North after a series of adulterous affairs on his part. This was supposed to be a *"let's start over"* season of our lives. There had been so much physical, emotional, spiritual, and psychological abuse in the South, I agreed to *"give it one more try"* up North. A fresh start where neither of us had a past. I was determined to make this work. So many had spoken against a successful marriage at ages sixteen and nineteen, but here we are four years later. Things looked as if they were going well, however, less than three months into this new venture, he comes in from work and says, *"I don't want to be married anymore but we have to stay together for the kid's sake. I have found someone else and you need to do the same."*

WHAT!!!! On comes depression, the deepest, darkest, scariest time of my life, thus far. I couldn't eat, couldn't sleep, couldn't stop crying. Those seeds of rejection, abandonment, betrayal, unloved, used, hopeless, and helpless were being watered and I didn't know how much longer I could take this. I was hours from checking myself into a mental hospital when a neighbor invited me to a Jazz event where I met someone.

Through a series of events, I found myself four months pregnant, not sure if my son belonged to my husband or this other person. I got my own place for the 1st time in my life along with my children and things were going well. The healing process had begun toward my husband and it appeared that maybe there was a chance of reconciliation. Then it happened, yet another woman pops up. *"DONE."* That's it. So much for this whole commitment thing. With bitterness in my heart from the continual disregard to my emotions, I decided to take control. I will just fulfill fleshly needs without commitment and there's a guy outside that can help me out with that. Hints the beginning of the year of Lee, as I call it. Yeah, this non-commitment thing didn't work out so well for me, my life is being threatened and I'm running from the consequences of my own sin.

Now here I am heading back to ML like a puppy with its tail tucked between its legs. His words from years prior vibrating in my head, *"Nobody's going to want you with kids," "You're only safe with me," "You are my wife until we die," "You must submit to me," "You can't do anything right."* Well, here I go again with the promise looming *"We will be a family again"* as my motivation. I arrive October 8th and head straight to the ER as my baby boy is now struggling to breathe since he had not had medicine for over twenty-four hrs. Determined to surprise ML, I didn't call anyone. After the ER visit, we proceeded to surprise him only to walk into the house and find him in bed with yet another woman...My heart sank! I hurried out of the house before he saw me or my reaction. How could this be?

As I pulled off, I flipped the mirror down to look at myself. There appeared to be words plastered on my forehead: failure, stupid, betrayed, unworthy of being loved, rejected, abandoned, used, hopeless, and helpless. I began to pray,

*Lord, even now, I know I am Your child. I am Your baby girl. You are a good good Father. You love me above anything I can ever imagine, and I worship You alone. You are amazing. You sit high and look low and love me too much to leave me where I am and for that Father, I say Thank You. Thank you for the blood of your Son, Jesus, that was shed for the forgiveness of my sins, to set me free, and to reverse the works of the devil. I confess that I have done things that You have commanded me not to do and I have not done all that You have commanded me to do and for this Father, I am truly sorry. I repent of my wicked ways by turning my heart, mind, and will toward you. I thank You Lord for your forgiveness and I choose to forgive myself. Now Father give me the grace to forgive ML and Lee that I may be set free and begin to heal. I don't feel loved right now. Please show me who you say I am. Show me my value and purpose. In Jesus name, I pray, Amen.*

The stress of all that had taken place in the previous days landed me in labor eight weeks early. I gave birth to a beautiful baby girl. The placenta had released from my uterus and was protruded through my cervix. A few hours more and she would have been stillborn due to a lack of oxygen and nutrients. I was all alone in a state where I'd been betrayed. How did I get here?

In the weeks to follow, the Lord would begin to heal my damaged emotions.

**He showed me my strength:**

1. I was twenty-two years old with four children, two are still nursing.

2. I've driven thirteen and a half hours with a one year old with asthma and no medication.

3. My baby's father is looking to kill me.

4. I caught my then husband in bed with another woman.

5. My baby is born pre-mature and could have died.

Yet, I'm getting ready to board a Greyhound bus alone with my babies to begin a new life some fifteen and a half hours away. The bus ride with four babies was interesting, but God let them sleep most of the time and sent angels to help me with bathroom breaks and diaper changes. While they slept, I cried and prayed.

Over everybody of water, I did what my Grandmother had taught me; *"toss all your cares, concerns, and worries into the water and allow it to take them far away."* I prayed, *"Father please break any ties I have to anyone from my past. Let me not desire to contact or communicate with anyone in Detroit or Georgia. I want to be free of those connections and be open to all you have for me in Oklahoma."* He told me to throw out my phonebook, yes, we still had those. I did. It was probably one of the hardest things to do, but I knew I couldn't move forward while looking through the rearview mirror. He was unlocking my Inner Warrior!

I arrived in Oklahoma with a new sense of humility took over as I was going back into my mothers' home as a married woman with four children. I returned as a child with childlike faith, totally submitted to whatever God had in store for me. Having a time to forgive all who had hurt me the healing of my soul was taking place and I was able to start really seeing myself through God's eyes.

In three short months I managed to get a job, my own place, and establish a church home. Shortly after I publicly rededicated my life and was rebaptized truly understanding what it meant to accepting Jesus as Lord, not just Savior.

I was not what I had done. I was not what others had called me. I was not what I had been through. I was who he said I was. I had returned to God and was identified with my creator who had determined my value and named me. He showed me who I was to Him, so I had to disown the lies I had believed about myself. This was my method of renewing my mind.

**I am completely Accepted in Christ, so I *"DISOWN"* the lie that I am rejected, unloved, dirty, or shameful.**

God says ...

*I am His child.*                                              John 1:12

*I've been grafted into His life.*                             John 15:15

*I've been declared forgiven of all my sins.*                  Romans 5:1

*I've been bought with a price and belong to Him.*
1 Corinthian 6:19-20

*I've been incorporated into Christ's body, the church.*
1 Corinthians 12:27

*I am seen as a saint, a holy one.*                            Ephesians 1:1

*I've been adopted as His child.*                  Ephesians 1:5

*I'm given access to Him through the Holy Spirit.*     Ephesians 2:18

## I am totally Secure in Christ, so I *"DISOWN"* the lie that I am guilty, unprotected, alone or abandoned.

God says ...

*He has freed me forever from condemnation.*       Romans 8:1-21

*He will work all things together for good.*          Romans 8:28

*He will never allow anything to separate me from His love.*
Romans 8:35-39

*He will complete to perfection the work He began in me.*
Philippians 1:6

*He has made me a citizen of heaven.*             Philippians 3:20

*He has not given me a spirit of fear.*               2 Timothy 1:7

*He will pour out grace and mercy in my time of need.*
Hebrews 4:16

*He will not let the evil one harm me. I am born of Him.*
1 John 5:18

## I am Significant in Christ, so I *"DISOWN"* the lie that I am unimportant, inadequate, incompetent, or powerless.

God says ...

*I've been chosen and appointed to bear fruit.*        John 15:16

*I've been empowered by His Spirit to be His witness.*

Acts 1:8

*I've been appointed as a minister of reconciliation.*
2 Corinthians 5:18

*I've been chosen to work with Him.*            2 Corinthians 6:1

*I've been seated with Christ in the heavenly realm.*
Ephesians 2:6

*I've been designed and crafted to do good works.*     Ephesians 2:10

*I may approach Him with freedom and confidence.*
Ephesians 3:12

*I can do all things through Christ who strengthens me!!*
Philippians 4:13

It was uphill from there. A warrior was born. I began to seek the face of the Lord to discover my purpose. It wasn't long before He revealed why He created me and every pain I had experienced had a purpose. They were strategically designed to prepare me for the ministry of helping hurting people heal from difficult life issues. To help individuals walk in their identity, get unstuck, and give birth to their purpose with confidence rightly placed in God.

You can unlock your Inner Warrior as well by identifying the lies, disowning them, and seeking the truth of who God says you are.

## STRATEGIES TO UNLOCK YOUR INNER WARRIOR

1. Who or what have you allowed to name you?

_____
_____
_____
_____
_____

2. Who or what has been allowed to determine your identity?

_____
_____
_____
_____
_____

3. Who or what has been allowed to determine your purpose

_____
_____
_____
_____
_____

4. Who or what has been allowed to determine your value?

_____
_____
_____
_____
_____

5. Have you returned to the Creator to find out your name, identity, purpose and value?

_____
_____
_____
_____
_____

6. What does the creator say about you?

_____
_____
_____
_____
_____

# ABOUT TAFFINEY NOLAN WILLIAMS

Born to teenage parents, Taffiney was adopted by her great aunt and raised as an only child in Jackson, Mississippi. From her mother's womb where she survived an attempted herbal abortion, she continues to be a testimony that God is STILL in the miracle-working business.

She lives her purpose by empowering, motivating, and encouraging people to be all that God has called them to be despite their past. She is known as an Inspirational Speaker, Life Coach, Discipleship Counselor, Preacher-Teacher, Spiritual Midwife, as well as a Best-Selling Author.

With over 17 years of ministry, she founded Journey to Impact Ministries, a team committed to helping people understand their value and identity in Christ. Through creative and innovate methods they provide resources promoting self-evaluation leading to healing and wholeness.

Taffiney is an Associate Minister of First Baptist Church of Murfreesboro, member of Artist in Christian Testimony, Inc. and Freedom in Christ Ministries which are active in over 80 countries worldwide. She resides with her husband Reginald in Murfreesboro, Tennessee. They are a blended family of 13 children and mentors to many.

For every 5 books sold, 1 will be donated to Shelters (battered, homeless), Recovery Centers, Confinement Institutions (jail, prison, half-way house), and Orphanages around the world

## CONTACT TAFFINEY

- Website: www.JourneyToImpact.org
- Facebook: www.Facebook.com/Journey2Impact
- Amazon: www.Amazon.com/author/taffineywilliams

# CHAPTER 16
# SONGS OF THE WARRIOR
By Tricia Andreassen

These songs where mentioned in my chapters of the book. I wanted to pass them on to you as you grow the Inner Warrior that is within you.

May these lyrics bless you and encourage you. The songs are available for purchase at: www.IgniteTheFireSongs.com

## WALK IN FAITH

**Verse:**
*Sometimes it can feel*
*Like your not moving forward*
*Trapped by your fear*
*You can't seem to get started*

*But that is when you close your eyes*
*To reach down in your soul*

*There you'll find*
*The strength you need*
*To take that journey*
*Meant for you*

**Chorus:**
*So walk in faith*
*Do not forget*
*How strong you are*

*If you just*
Can believe
*You will become*
*Who you are*

**Verse:**
*As you walk*
*On the path of life's future*
*It will arise*
*Is this really my destiny?*

*But that is when you close your eyes*
*To reach down in your soul*

*There you'll find*
*The strength you need*
*To take the journey meant for you*[4]

Lyrics by Tricia Andreassen

# YOU'RE NEVER TO OLD

**Verse:**
*My Momma told me*
*You should have started for your dream*
*When you were seventeen*

*But I didn't know then*
*How I'd feel today*
*I feel, yes, I feel today*

**Chorus:**
*You're never to old*
*To get your story told*
*To find a way*
*and make it your day*

*It's never to late*
*To discover your fate*
*To figure it out*
*What life's all about*

**Verse:**
*And after all these years*
*It's all coming clear*
*That it's not what others think*

*It's the health you have*
*And the Love you've found*
*That keeps it comin' round*

**Chorus:**
*You're never to old
To get your story told
To find a way
and make it your day*

*It's never to late
To discover your fate
To figure it out
What life's all about*[4]

Lyrics by Tricia Andreassen

# DREAMS FOR TOMORROW

**Verse:**
*Wakin up at 3*
*With a feelin' to be free*
*It's all you can know*

*You have to write it down*
*To feel your heart is found*
*It's your dreams for tomorrow*

**Chorus:**
*Don't wish your life away*
*Just cherish every day*
*Life's movin' forward*

*It's all up to you*
*You know it to be true*
*To keep pressin' onward*

**Verse:**
*You feel it in your heart*
*The tug at your soul*
*To make your dreams happen*

*It's the knowin' that you feel*
*That can make them all real*
*It's your dreams for tomorrow*

**Verse:**
*You've started down the path*
*Now there's no turning back*
*To what lies ahead*

*You just gotta believe*
*That its all meant to be*
*Its your dreams for tomorrow*[4]

Lyrics by Tricia Andreassen

# SAY YOUR PRAYERS

**Verse:**
*Finding hope can be hard when you're feelin' alone*
*Thinking back on the times*
*to know that you have grown*
*But you gotta' understand*
*That its all within His hands*
*He's the one that helps you stand*
*He's the one that holds your hand*

**Chorus:**
*Through the time and through the years*
*He's been the one to calm my fears*
*It's an age-old remedy*
*Say your prayers and let them be*
*Need not to fret, cause' I don't know*
*What the future will bring and what tomorrow may hold*

**Verse:**
*So when you feel you lost your way*
*Just remember everyday*
*That the simple plan to take*
*Is to pray through the day*
*And when you do*
*You'll start to feel*
*What's imagined can be real*
*That's the peace that you find*
*Through the darkness of the night*

**Chorus:**
*Through the time and through the years*
*He's been the one to calm my fears*
*It's an age-old remedy*

*Say your prayers and let them be*
*Need not to fret, cause' I don't know*
*What the future will bring and what tomorrow may hold*[4]

Lyrics by Tricia Andreassen

# SHIFT

**Chorus:**
*No longer want to just survive*
*I want my business to thrive*
*High on life is how I feel*
*When I know my dreams and I make them real.*

**Verse:**
*When I make that shift, I'll feel that lift*
*It's what I gotta do*
*I'm gonna climb so high that I'll touch the sky*
*And see my purpose shine*

**Chorus:**
*No longer want to just survive*
*I want my business to thrive*
*High on life is how I feel*
*When I know my dreams and I make them real.*

**Verse:**
*It's the path I take that will create this shift within my soul*
*It'll carry through*
*All to me and you*
*It's the mindset for us all*

**Chorus:**
*No longer want to just survive*
*We know our business will thrive*
*High on life is how we feel*
*Cause we know our dreams*
*And they now they're real*[4]

Lyrics by Tricia Andreassen

# ENDNOTES

[1]Songwriters: Linda Creed / Michael Masser
Greatest Love of All lyrics © Sony/ATV Music Publishing LLC

[2]Songwriters: MARTHA D MUNIZZI / DANIEL S MUNIZZI
Because of Who You Are lyrics © Say The Name Publishing

[3]Songwriters: Hannah Kerr
Warrior Song lyrics © Sawyer Brown's Mark Miller

[4]Songwriters: Tricia Andreassen
Produced by: Daniel Grimmett & Tricia Andreassen
On the CD itself: 2009© Tricia Andreassen. All rights reserved. Unauthorized duplication is a violation of applicable laws.

www.ingramcontent.com/pod-product-compliance
Lightning Source LLC
Chambersburg PA
CBHW071317110526
44591CB00010B/920